HIGH
SCHOOL
FOOTBALL

COLLEGE
FOOTBALL

Moving the Chains

A Parent's Guide to High School Football Recruiting

BY

Dr. Todd S. Meiklejohn

RECRUITING DOCTOR.COM
PUBLICATIONS

Contents

Chapter 5

The Importance of a Quality Highlight Film   **58**

Chapter 6

Contacting Coaches and Marketing Your Son   **66**

Chapter 7

Combines and Football Camps   **82**

Dedication

First and foremost, I dedicate this book to every parent who has sacrificed some part of their life to support their child's dreams and athletic aspirations. Including my own— Ellen and Bill. Thank you also to my beloved sisters Amy and Anne.

Secondly, I dedicate this book to Tia Broadway for all of her contributions and input, and to my three beautiful and talented children—Perry, Sydney, and Halley. This book would not be possible without your love, sacrifice and support.

Thank you to all of my coaches throughout the years—especially Don Soldinger and Willie Jeffries; as well as, to Bob Stinson for mentoring me and teaching me how to be an effective educational leader.

Special thanks to RDR charter member and visionary "coach" Noah Wilbanks for supporting RDR's vision and mission from its inception and to Shannon Sejeck for all his years of friendship and support.

My sincerest gratitude and appreciation to coach Dave Kelly for being a friend, a mentor and for sharing his insights. He is a 'class act' and represents the future of college coaching.

Finally, I dedicate this book to Madeline Mendez and thank her for her contributions, her patience and sacrifices to ensure that not only this book became a reality, but also RDR. TQM

Chapter 1

What You Should Know Before You Begin the Recruiting Process

"Football is like life—it requires perseverance, self-denial, hard work, sacrifice, dedication and respect for authority."

Vince Lombardi
Legendary NFL coach,
Five time NFL champion

Today, the competition for football scholarships is fierce; there really are not many full scholarship opportunities available each year for high school athletes and the odds of a receiving a scholarship are slim. In addition, the football recruiting process is not an exact science; the rules change from year to year, athletes must start early and there is no margin for error. For every football player who signs a scholarship on national signing day each year, there are tens of thousands more that sit at home watching TV left wondering, "What happened to me and why didn't I receive a scholarship?"

In all honesty, there is a lot of recruiting information out there and many different recruiting guides on the market, containing a lot of different information that can be confusing. However, do not panic because you have chosen the right resource to help you and your son. This guide and its content are written specifically for the football recruiting process and just for **YOU** (THE PARENT)—*the greatest asset in your son's recruiting process*! The information contained in this book is relevant, up-to-date, easy to understand and there are numerous recruiting tips and strategies that you can immediately make use of to assist your son and help him succeed with his recruiting efforts. This book also includes many proven recruiting dos and don'ts, vital academic strategies, all of today's NCAA eligibility information, essential recruiting terminology, useful websites, and 'interactive' recruiting tools so that your son can avoid today's most common recruiting mistakes. Best of all, you can read this book in less than one day and learn how to take a proactive (do-it-yourself) approach to today's multifaceted recruiting process, how to develop a comprehensive four-year recruiting plan specific to your son's ability and how to effectively promote him to the right colleges. Finally, you will benefit from the insights of an author who currently works with athletes in the football recruiting process and who has experienced this process as a player, a coach, an educator and as a parent.

How Many Football Scholarships are Available

There are almost one million prospective high school student-athletes who participate in organized football throughout the country each year. Approximately 300,000, or 30%, of those competing are seniors. However, as reflected in Table 1 on the next page, there are on average only about 6,700 Division I and Division I-AA football scholarships available each year and only about 12,000 additional football scholarship opportunities (either full or partial) divided between the Division II, NAIA, and junior college levels. Although the figures represented in Table 1 are averages, the total number of scholarship opportunities each year fluctuates and can significantly decrease once you factor in the number of scholarships actually available for incoming players at each school and at each division level. It is important to note that institutions at the lower division levels "split" their available monies into what is known as a *partial scholarship*, or an athletic scholarship that only covers a specific portion of an athlete's tuition, university fees, textbooks and/or room and board expenses. Either way, when you do the mental math, you may have 300,000 potential high school football players each year competing for only about 20,000 college scholarship opportunities. Given these odds, you begin to realize just how difficult it might be for your son to actually receive a full scholarship and how fortunate he truly is if he does.

Table 1 *Available Scholarship Opportunities by Competition Level*

Division	Number of Institutions	Total Roster Scholarships Allowed per Team Each Year	Incoming Scholarships Allowed	Total Incoming Scholarships Available Per Year
NCAA (D1) Football Bowl Subdivision (FBS)	120	85	Up to 25	3,000
NCAA (1-AA) Football Championship Subdivision (FCS)	125	63	Up to 30	3,750
NCAA Division II	156	36	36	5,616
National Association of Intercollegiate Athletics (NAIA)	92	24	24	2,208
National Junior College Athletic Association	68	85	85	5,780
			TOTAL	20,354

The pie graph on the next page better illustrates just how many seniors on average actually receive either a full football scholarship or some type of partial athletic scholarship to play football in college each year. This equates to:

- Less than one percent (or about 3,000) of all graduating high school seniors receive an NCAA Division I (FBS) full scholarship.
- Another one percent (or about 3,700) receives an NCAA Division I-AA (FCS) full scholarship.
- Only about five percent more (or about 12,000) of the rest of the playing population receives some form of partial athletic financial assistance to play either at the Division II, NAIA, or NJCAA (junior college) level.

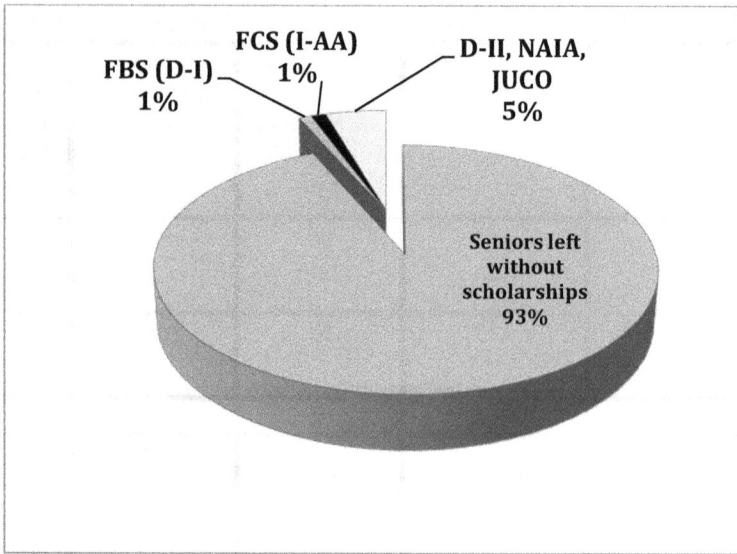

Figure 1. Average Yearly Football Scholarship Opportunities

On average each year, only one percent of all high school senior football players actually sign a full scholarship and another six percent receive some type of partial scholarship assistance. This means, *93% of the remaining eligible playing population will not receive any form of athletic assistance whatsoever.* Suffice it to say, most people know little about the specific scholarship numbers, or the slim odds of obtaining a scholarship. I would venture to say that you have chosen to read this book to learn about how the high school football recruiting process actually works and how this book can assist your son.

Common Recruiting Mistakes

Procrastination is the biggest mistake you or your son can make in the recruiting process since the majority of Division I football prospects are identified by the end of their sophomore year. Please believe me when I tell you that your son's senior year is not the optimal time to start his recruiting process or to begin pulling out all of the stops in order to help him get noticed by college recruiters. While grades and ability will be paramount in determining if your son obtains a scholarship, it is essential that he avoid these *common recruiting mistakes* during his recruiting process:

- Waiting too long to begin the recruiting process
- Not having a recruiting plan tailored to his abilities
- Not targeting compatible or realistic schools that match his ability level
- Not knowing where to find the right recruiting resources or finding them too late
- Falling into a false sense of security that colleges will automatically find him and offer him a scholarship because he received a few general recruiting letters
- Not having a quality highlight film (or game film), not sending it to schools upon request, or sending a poor quality highlight film to a college recruiter
- Reluctance to utilize all available recruiting resources
- Ignoring college correspondence and invitations to visit their campus
- Failure to build/not knowing how to build a recruiting relationship
- Not promoting or marketing himself online and to the recruiting media

In order to avoid these common mistakes, there are *ten key recruiting objectives* that will directly benefit your son with his recruiting efforts and which you will master after reading this book. Those strategies are:

1. Learning how to develop a recruiting plan specific to your son's abilities.
2. Knowing when, where, and how to effectively market your son to college recruiters, how to contact them and build recruiting relationships.
3. Knowing how to determine your son's recruiting needs.
4. Determining which level of college football is right for his ability.
5. Knowing how many football scholarship opportunities are available to your son.
6. Becoming familiar with all of the current NCAA eligibility and recruiting guidelines.
7. Knowing exactly what is required for your son to become an

NCAA "qualifier".

8. Knowing how to successfully monitor your son's academic progress.

9. Knowing how to develop a quality highlight film.

10. Knowing where you can find other forms of financial college assistance for your son in case he does not receive an athletic scholarship.

Again, this book not only contains numerous strategies to address these items, but also to help you ensure that your son maximizes his recruiting efforts and avoids today's most common recruiting mistakes.

The Business of Football Recruiting

Today, the competition in college football recruiting is fierce, and high school football is a multi-million dollar business. Large brand-name companies are now sponsoring high school events such as combines and football camps, and national media outlets such as ESPN devote prime-time network coverage to regular season high school games, annual All-American games, and to the most widely televised day of the year, "national signing day". Recruiting is a year-round business in the college coaching ranks and the head coach and his staff's job security rest heavily upon, first and foremost, winning football games, but also on how well they recruit and produce on national signing day each year! In the world of major college football, the primary goal each year is to make it into the Bowl Championship Series (BCS) rankings, to its national championship game, or to any other number of post-season bowl games sponsored by companies that award a huge payday to their selected universities. Simply put, building a winning or championship football program directly correlates with consistently landing the most talented recruits available each year. Due to this tremendous pressure to recruit and win year-after-year, it is not surprising that middle school prospects are now being closely monitored and evaluated. In June of 2010, the landscape of college recruiting intensified even further when the University of Nebraska agreed to join the Big Ten Conference, which formed college football's first "Super Conference." This bold move prompted several other institutions to either leave, or consider leaving, their traditional football conferences for a rival or higher profile conference. In the near future, college football conference realignment will not only intensify football recruiting, but it will also have significant financial implications on college football for years to come.

Most of my life, I have been involved in one way or another with high school football as a player, a coach, a life-long educator and as a parent. Suffice it to say, many of the recruiting strategies incorporated throughout this guide were derived from my field experience directly assisting athletes, listening to parents and athletes, gathering their feedback, personally observing the perils associated with the recruiting process, and obviously through research. Please make use of this book to its fullest, utilize its many strategies and interactive elements and please refer the book to a family member or friend.

I thank you for choosing to read this book; I hope you find it easy to read and I hope it is a useful recruiting tool that assists you and your son. I also applaud you for your commitment toward taking a proactive approach to helping your son succeed with his recruiting efforts and to helping him achieve his dream of playing college football. By choosing to read this guide, you have made a wise investment into your son's future. If we can assist you or your son in any way, simply visit us on the Web at **www.recruitingdoctor.com**

RDR

RECRUITING DOCTOR.COM

Chapter 2
The Six Components of a Recruiting Plan

"Make sure your recruiting journey and your recruiting plan has both a 'take off' and a 'landing."

Dr. Todd S. Meiklejohn

Besides procrastination, the second most common mistake that parents make in the recruiting process is that they do not have a recruiting plan. It is a mistake to wait around passively thinking that schools are going to "discover" your son, aggressively recruit him, and/or think that a scholarship offer is a certainty and will somehow arrive in the mail his senior year. Never assume that colleges know about your son, know how to find him, or that he is on their recruiting "radar". No matter how many people (including college coaches) tell your son how good he is, how high he is ranked by the recruiting media, how many times he's featured in the local newspaper, how many awards he's won, or how many records he's broken, he can still go unnoticed by colleges and ultimately go without a scholarship (or scholarship offer).

RECRUITING TIP: The ultimate goal of your son's recruiting plan is to develop **one** successful recruiting relationship and get **one** school to fall in love with him since in reality; he is only able to sign **one** scholarship offer.

On the other hand, athletes and their parents can fall into a false sense of security when they receive a few general letters of interest from colleges. General football correspondence is nothing more than a formatted letter from a school containing information about the school's program, maybe a questionnaire, or a note from the coach stating that your son has been "identified" or "recommended" as a prospect for them to target. Although receiving correspondence is a good recruiting sign, do not get too overjoyed about general football correspondence since colleges send out thousands of these formatted letters to prospects across the country each year, and there are thousands of players opening that same exact letter as your son. If a questionnaire is enclosed, chances are the school knows little (or nothing) about your son and does not have any pertinent information about him in their recruiting database. On the other hand, receiving a questionnaire is actually a good thing, an important part in building a recruiting relationship and a key data-gathering instrument used by colleges to obtain a prospect's current academic, personal and athletic information. Therefore, *always follow up by filling out the questionnaire and placing it back into the mail within twenty-four hours.* We will cover "correspondence" and "contact" in more detail later in Chapter 6, but always remember that *each time you reach out to a school it creates the opportunity to build a recruiting relationship, which could lead to a phone call from a coach, an invitation to the school, or even a formal written offer*—your ultimate goal.

Component 1: Assessing Your Son's Recruiting Needs

Now that we have established the importance of your son having a recruiting plan and starting early, his recruiting plan should be diversified and specific to his abilities! The first step to creating your son's recruiting plan involves you and your son evaluating his recruiting needs which considers: 1) determining where he actually is in his recruiting process versus where he should be, 2) knowing where to focus your recruiting efforts and 3) deciding if he requires recruiting assistance. Furthermore, you must objectively assess his actual abilities both academically and athletically, determine which level of college football competition is best for him, set realistic expectations, know all of today's current recruiting rules and NCAA eligibility requirements and then match your son's abilities to a schools specific needs.

Since this is not an exact science, how can you effectively determine if your son is (or is not) being 'actively' or 'seriously' recruited? How will you know where to focus your recruiting efforts and more importantly—where should you begin? In other words, how do you begin to assess your sons recruiting needs? A good first step is to sit down with your son and complete The RDR Recruiting Assessment on the next page. This assessment will help you address these important questions; as well as, assist you in the formulation of your son's recruiting plan.

Table 2 *The RDR Recruiting Assessment*

Y	N	Recruiting Assessment
		Does your son have a recruiting plan?
		Does he have any verbal or written scholarship offers?
		Has he received phone calls from coaches (only answer if he is a junior or senior)?
		Has he received a steady stream of "hand written" letters from coaches (not questionnaires, form letters, or generic letters from colleges)?
		Has he received any invitations from colleges to visit their campus for events such as a Junior Day, or to attend a Spring game or regular season football game(s)?
		Does he have a highlight film?
		Does he have a player profile?
		Has he received any invitations and brochures from colleges to attend their summer camp?
		Are coaches attending his school practices or games to specifically scout him when permitted by the NCAA?
		Have colleges requested copies of his transcripts and test scores?
		Has he taken any un-official visits to schools?
		Has he read the NCAA's *Guide for the College Bound Athlete*?
		Has he set his academic and athletic goals for the year?
		Have you and he identified his core course requirements and ensured he is taking classes from his high school's list of approved NCAA core courses?
		Has he met with his guidance counselor to determine the courses required to graduate in eight semesters?
		Has he sought out recruiting advice from his head coach for recruiting tips and feedback?

If your son is able to answer "YES" to a majority of the assessment questions outlined above, he has good grades, and if it is early enough in his recruiting process, then he may be ahead of the game and on track towards receiving a scholarship. On the other hand, if he answered "NO" to a majority of these questions, then your son *IS NOT ON ANYONES RECRUITNG RADAR AND HE NEEDS TO INTENSIFY HIS RECRUITNG EFFORTS.* It bears repeating that if your son is not academically qualified and does not officially have a written scholarship offer; do not proceed casually in your recruiting efforts. He may be in jeopardy of not receiving a scholarship.

The Four-Year RDR Recruiting Progression Plan (RPP)

To further assist you in determining your son's recruiting needs, what you should be doing to assist him and further define where he should be with his recruiting progression as opposed to where he actually is, I developed a four year recruiting plan called the RDR Recruiting Progression Plan (RPP) outlined in Appendixes F to I. Like the assessment above, the RPP details specific recruiting strategies and objectives that your son should be accomplishing from his freshman year all the way through his senior year and up to national signing day. Keep in mind that the RPP is not intended to be an all-inclusive plan designed to exactly match all of your son's recruiting needs, but more of a blue-print to provide him with specific recruiting strategies and objectives to accomplish; as well as, help you assess his recruiting needs and develop his individualized recruiting plan.

With the advancements in recruiting technology and the trend shifting to now include monitoring and evaluating middle school prospects, your son must 'sprint out of the blocks' with his recruiting efforts the moment he enters the ninth grade. As reflected in the RPP, there is a lot to be accomplished during his freshman and sophomore year, with respect to preparation and planning for his physical and academic development as a student-athlete. A 'student-athlete' (prospective student-athlete) is defined as any athlete who participates in an organized competitive sport sponsored by the educational institution in which he or she is enrolled. During your son's freshman year set his academic goals high to make certain he becomes eligible for a scholarship, begin to research all levels of college football competition, decide upon a few local schools to target and begin to focus realistically on what level of college football is right for him. Important freshman recruiting objectives include:

(1) Developing your son's recruiting plan for the year.
(2) Setting his academic goals.
(3) Attending combines, camps and/or specialized football speed or skills training to improve his strength and develop his football skills sets.
(4) Targeting, contacting and visiting nearby schools.
(5) Becoming familiar with the NCAA's current recruiting and eligibility guidelines.

IMPORTANT NCAA RULE: During a student-athlete's freshman and sophomore years, the NCAA does not permit coaches to call either the athlete or their parent(s), nor have off-campus contact with either, but they may send the athlete camp brochures, questionnaires or general college admission information. However, the athlete and their parent(s) may initiate any form of contact with a college or university at anytime beginning in the athlete's freshman year.

On September 1st of your son's junior year, the recruiting rules change, as coaches are permitted to contact him more freely by phone and by mail. By this time, his recruiting efforts should begin to crystallize and be much more specific. In fact, he should be in good academic standing, registered for the NCAA's Clearinghouse, eligible for an NCAA scholarship, receiving serious college correspondence, being evaluated by college coaches, have a solid athletic resume, player profile and a quality highlight film. With all of these variables aligning, your son may even start receiving and/or have scholarship offers and his goal of playing at the college level will be closer than ever to reality.

Component 2: Determining What Level of College Football is Right for Your Son.

The second component to consider in the development of your son's recruiting plan is which colleges or universities he should realistically target and which level of college football competition is right for him. This determination is primarily based upon his athletic and academic ability, but you may also consider which geographical part of the country he feels most comfortable playing in (if he has the option of offers to play out- of-state), and which position that he is being actively recruited to play in college. In your determination as to which colleges to target, consider:

- Your son's academic ability and grade point average.
- How many years your son was a starter at the varsity level.
- Whether your son is one of the best players on the team or at his position.
- How his abilities compare to others in his league, city, or state.
- Which football division levels are currently targeting him or seriously recruiting him.
- His coach's feedback and evaluation.
- Your son's entire body of work on the field (his statistics, awards, etc.).
- How he will socially adapt at the school.
- The location(s) of the school(s).
- Whether these colleges and universities are actively and/or seriously recruiting him.

When evaluating your son, be realistic about his actual ability level. All too often, parents, close friends and even coaches are biased to an athlete's ability and tend to conclude that the player is more talented than they actually are. What you as a parent must first realize and accept is that not every athlete can play at the Division I level and that your son may not have the ability to play at the Division I level, nor develop into a top-rated prospect and be aggressively recruited by multiple schools. You and your son should never compare his abilities to other prospects since his recruiting path will differ and he will have his own recruiting plan specific to his ability level, circumstances, and academic standing. I am sure that every prospect's goal (and parent's desire) is geared toward playing at the Division I football level, obtaining a full four-year football scholarship and playing in front of a sold-out crowd on national television. However, we have already noted that these scholarship opportunities are scarce, competition is fierce and, for a number of reasons already noted, your son may not have the ability, the grades, or the necessary combination of both to land a full athletic scholarship. Do not panic, there are several division levels that do award athletic scholarships and that may be a perfect fit for your son. As you evaluate and consider what playing level and which school is right for your son, keep in mind that your ultimate goals are to:

1. Get at least one school to fall in love with him and offer him a scholarship.
2. Find the right school that fits his athletic and academic abilities.
3. Find a school he feels comfortable at and that feels like 'home'.
4. Ensure he receives a college education.

Ultimately, have him keep his options open, put egos aside, gather all of the information available to you, and explore every available playing level and option available to him.

NCAA College Football Divisions

The NCAA consists of four football divisions. The most widely recognized and highest level of college football competition is the NCAA's Football Bowl Subdivision (FBS), formerly known as, but still referred to as Division I (D1). It is also the only NCAA-sponsored sport without an organized tournament to determine its national football champion. Instead, schools in the FBS compete in the highly lucrative Bowl Championship Series (BCS) to determine a national football champion, while other BCS schools compete for invitations to numerous other post-season bowl games. As of 2009, there were 120 football institution members of the NCAA's FBS and each institution is limited to a total of eighty-five football players receiving financial assistance. That assistance includes both partial and full scholarships (The NCAA, "Division Levels", 2010). An athlete receiving a partial scholarship at an FBS school counts fully against the total number of eighty-five scholarships. The service academies, which include the Army, Navy, and Air Force, are exempt from this rule, and all of their students receive full scholarships through the U.S. government that are paid for by U.S. taxpayers.

The second highest level of Division I football is the Football Championship Subdivision (FCS), also commonly referred to as Division I-AA. Unlike the FBS, the FCS determines its annual football champion in a twenty-team, single-elimination tournament. A few Championship Subdivision conferences are composed of schools that offer no athletic scholarships at all, most notably the Ivy League and the Pioneer Football League, a football-only conference. The Patriot League also does not award football scholarships, but permits them in other sports (athletes receiving these scholarships are ineligible to play football for Patriot League schools). On the other hand, the Northeast Conference began offering a maximum of thirty full scholarship equivalents in 2006 (which will grow to forty by 2011 after a later vote of the league's school presidents and athletic directors).

The NCAA Division II (or D-II) level is the intermediate-division level of football competition (third level) in which the schools tend to be smaller public universities and many private institutions. Athletic scholarships are offered at most Division II institutions, but with more stringent limits to the numbers offered in any one sport, compared to the Division I level. For example, Division II schools are limited to only thirty-six football scholarships, whereas Division I FBS are allowed eighty-five football scholarships. It is common for a Division I student-athlete to transfer to a D-II schools since the transferring student-athlete may receive not only a scholarship, but they also do not have to sit out a year before resuming sports participation, as would be the case if a student was transferring from one Division I institution to another (Football players transferring from a Division I FBS school to a Division I FCS school also do not have to sit out a year.). Currently there are 282 full and/or provisional members of Division II (The NCAA, "Division Levels", 2010). Similar to the FCS (I-AA) level, there is an annual national single-elimination tournament to determine its football national champion. To learn more about playing at the D-II level, their affiliating schools, and the latest D-II football news, visit http://www.d2football.com.

The final NCAA level of football competition is the Division III (D-III) level. The D-III competition level consists of colleges and universities that essentially do not offer athletically related financial aid (athletic scholarships) to their student-athletes, since athletics is considered a non-revenue making extracurricular activity for students. However, most athletes competing at the D-III level are on some form of financial assistance that covers most or all of their yearly tuition and expenses, which is why this is a viable college option for those players who may not secure a full four-year scholarship.

There are 449 member institutions, which makes D-III the largest of the three divisions sanctioned by the NCAA. However, only about 230 schools actually field a football team. Division III schools range in size from less than five hundred to over ten thousand students. Division III institutions are not permitted to redshirt freshmen athletes as is typical at the Division I level, and they may not use endowments or funds to benefit their athletic programs (The NCAA, "Division Levels", 2010). Normally, athletes are granted four years of eligibility to compete and obtain their bachelor's degree. To find out more about the D-III football level, visit www.d3football.com. For specific information and the complete rules and regulations for each NCAA playing level, visit www.ncaa.org

The National Association of Intercollegiate Athletics (NAIA)

Playing at the NAIA level is an alternative to NCAA schools. The eligibility requirements for playing at the NAIA level are different from those of the NCAA. The NAIA level in terms of school size and football competition is often compared to the NCAA's Division III level in that the colleges and universities are smaller and academically focused. Several offer some type of athletic scholarship; however, do not expect a full scholarship. Advantages for student-athletes competing at the NAIA level may include more playing time, and certainly more opportunity to access scholarship money.

Here are five (5) important things to know about the NAIA and their available scholarships:

1. The NAIA currently has *no clearinghouse*, unlike the NCAA Eligibility Center. However, they will institute their own version of an Eligibility Center/Clearinghouse beginning in the 2011-12 school year. The NAIA and NCAA Clearinghouses are two separate entities and certification of NAIA eligibility is separate from NCAA eligibility.

2. The current NAIA eligibility requirements include:
   - Graduating from high school, and
   - Meeting two of the following three criteria: (1) have an ACT test score of at least 18 or an SAT score of at least 860, (2) have a GPA of at least 2.0, or (3) finish in the top half of your graduating class.

3. There are a *limited number of scholarships*. As with the NCAA, teams are only allowed up to twenty-four (24) football scholarships each year, but that does not mean that the college will necessarily have them available each year. Most NAIA athletes are awarded partial athletic scholarships (on average $7000) in addition to financial aid or a need based academic scholarship.

4. *What counts as an athletic scholarship?* Any money you receive from the school, including athletic grants (or scholarships), academic scholarships, leadership or performance awards, outside scholarships administered by the institution, and tuition waivers are considered athletic scholarships.

5. *What does not count as an athletic scholarship?* NAIA scholarships that are not considered athletic aid are, scholarships "that are not funded, controlled, or allocated in any significant way by the institution." These include federal loans and Pell grants.

To learn more about NAIA member institutions and the current eligibility requirements, visit their official Web site http://naia.cstv.com.

The Junior College Level

The junior college football level, also known in football circles as "JUCO," is a two-year college option available to athletes prior to attending a four-year college. Generally, athletes who take this route did not meet NCAA eligibility standards for a full scholarship, may have been overlooked during the recruiting process, or may have gotten into some type of trouble during high school that jeopardized their chances for a scholarship. The National Junior College Athletic Association (NJCAA; http://www.njcaa.org) is divided into sixteen regions of competition across the country, and is the largest governing body of junior college athletics for both men's and women's sports. In the state of California, the California Community College Athletic Association (CCCAA; http://www.coasports.org) fields numerous football programs and competes at a highly competitive junior college football level. So, if need be, search around for all of the JUCO football options.

Prep School or Military Academy Option

This post-high school option is reserved for a student-athlete that either did not graduate from high school in the required four-year period (eight academic semesters) or may need an extra year of high school to meet the NCAA's eligibility requirements. While attending a prep or military school, a student-athlete does not lose college eligibility since they will utilize a fifth year of high school to compete in their selected sport, improve their core course GPA and improve their ACT or SAT score. It is important to note that a student-athletes high school GPA is locked in this option and can only be improved by retaking courses. The ultimate goal of a student-athlete attending a prep or military school is to receive their high school diploma and meet all NCAA's eligibility requirements.

However, some athlete's leave this option having achieved only one of these goals and/or without achieving either. In this case, the NCAA classifies them as either a "non-qualifier" or a "partial-qualifier". Any student-athlete entering an NCAA institution is considered a *non-qualifier* if they did not graduate from high school or did not obtain the required core grade point average and SAT or ACT score. A non-qualifier is not permitted to attend team practices, participate in any competitions for one full academic year at their institution or receive an athletic scholarship. However, they may apply for and receive need-based financial aid. On the other hand, a *partial qualifier* is a student-athlete who, at the time of graduation from high school obtained *one* of the following: the required number of core courses, the required core grade-point average in the core curriculum, or the minimum SAT or ACT score. A partial qualifier is eligible to practice and may receive an athletic scholarship, but may not compete in any competitions during their first academic year. Chapter 4 will detail all of the NCAA's eligibility requirements in order to become a *'qualifier'*.

Now that you have a general understanding about the various football options available to your son, the discussions and decision as to which level of college football is right for him, what option he will pursue, and which institution he will attend is not a decision that should be taken lightly. In fact, his decision will not only have an impact upon his immediate future, but will also affect the rest of his life. For this reason, I recommend your conversations be extremely "personal," include your closest family members, and include input from his head coach and/or other qualified individuals you trust. Consulting your son's head coach to assess his chances for a scholarship and gauging his involvement level in your son's recruiting process is a critical component to developing his recruiting plan. However, if his head coach provides him with little or no feedback, seems skeptical about his chances or ability for a scholarship, and/or is simply not involved in his recruiting process, do not argue the point or get discouraged. If your son truly has the desire to play at the next level, tell him to set his goals high and stay true to his dream, regardless of what others may say.

If you are unable to iron out these details, it bears repeating that you should seek input from a qualified and trusted third-party source that can help you accurately assess your son's ability level and help him develop a recruiting plan specific to his needs and abilities. In addition, during your initial conversations about which level of college football is best for him, engage in thorough discussions with your son pertaining to all of the important aspects about his grades and the

NCAA's eligibility standards needed to qualify for an athletic scholarship. Ultimately, be realistic about your son's abilities, keep his options open, plan effectively, and there will be a college team and level of college football that is right for him in the end.

Component 3: Considering Your Sons Academic Abilities

One very important aspect that parents overlook when determining their son's probability of receiving an athletic scholarship is his true academic ability in relation to becoming qualified for an athletic scholarship. In order to assist your son academically during high school and increase his chances of becoming eligible to receive an athletic scholarship, incorporate the **academic strategies** outlined below when developing his recruiting plan:

1. Formulate and set his academic goals prior to each school year.
2. Assess your son's need for subject-specific tutoring and find out who provides such services at his high school.
3. Know his required NCAA core courses and ensure that he is taking the exact classes that match his high school's list of approved NCAA core courses.
4. Know how to calculate your son's "core" grade point average (core GPA) (refer to the appendices A and B) and his *weighted* and *un-weighted* GPA; as well as, teach him how to calculate all three.
5. Ensure he maintains at least a 3.0 core GPA throughout high school.
6. Ensure he graduates on time and in eight academic semesters.
7. Provide him with SAT/ACT prep tutoring and know the scheduled exam dates (check for free ACT/SAT tutoring).
8. Always know his current class schedule, the names of his teacher's and their contact information.
9. Know the name and contact information of his guidance counselor, the school's athletic guidance counselor, and the schools athletics director.
10. Know all of the NCAA's current eligibility standards.
11. Conduct regular transcript analyses with his guidance counselor in order to monitor and assess his academic standing.

Finding information to these important academic objectives and other vital NCAA eligibility requirements can be a daunting task for most parents, but do not panic! This guide conveniently covers the points outlined above, the NCAA's current eligibility requirements and provides you with plenty of strategies in Chapter 4 to support your son academically throughout high school.

As a life-long educator, I've always subscribed to the motto of 'academics first' so keep in mind that as your son progresses through high school and signing day draws near, his probability for a scholarship can significantly increase or decrease, depending upon whether or not he meets NCAA eligibility standards or he actually has the ability to become eligible.

> **ACADEMIC TIP**: The higher your son's GPA is throughout high school and the sooner he is officially 'eligible' by the NCAA's standards, the better his chances are for a scholarship.

Also keep in mind that Division I eligibility requirements are completely different from the other football divisions and the NAIA's requirements. We all hear the horror stories of the gifted athlete that loses their scholarship when they do not academically qualify or when a college passes on them due to their poor performance in the classroom. Do not let this story be the sad ending to your son's football career and dreams of a college education!

Component 4: Determining if Your Son Needs Recruiting Assistance

After you have realistically determined where your son is with his recruiting efforts, you have decided what competition level matches both his playing ability and academic ability, you must consider whether he may need recruiting assistance. A recruiting professional, or effective third-party source can teach you how to market you son's abilities to recruiters and help him to navigate successfully through the pit-falls of the recruiting process. While third-party recruiting assistance may not be necessary for every prospect, it may prove invaluable to you and your son if it is from an experienced and trusted source. Always remember that no one can provide you and your son with all of the recruiting answers, *nor can anyone guarantee your son a scholarship*. There are also some "crooks" in this business and "snake-oil salesmen" who prey on people's desperation, tell lies, charge enormously high fees and dole out *bad* recruiting advice. So before you begin your search for assistance or pay for it, consider this before you make a decision:

RECRUITING TIP: If you needed legal advice, you would go to a trusted lawyer; if you needed medical advice, you would always attempt to choose the best doctor. Therefore, when you seek recruiting advice or assistance, utilize the same rationale and ensure that it is from a qualified, trusted and competent source.

Over the years, I have met many parents who were resourceful in their own right and on target with their son's recruiting efforts. On the other hand, many desperately needed information, assistance, advice, and guidance. Remember that the NCAA's recruiting rules constantly change and are not what they were two years ago, much less five or ten years ago. In addition, the recruiting process today is multi-faceted and not an exact science. All too often, parents and athletes receive bad recruiting advice from people who know little or nothing about today's football recruiting process or the current recruiting guidelines. On the other hand, many parents are reluctant to seek recruiting help from a third-party source and find themselves with the heartbreaking reality that their son has neither any scholarship offers— the offers that they had hoped to receive—nor any time left, as signing day has passed and graduation day draws nears.

Which Type of Recruiting Service is Right for Your Son?

So what types of recruiting services are available to your son and which one is right for him? Choosing a person or recruiting service to assist you and one that is right for him primarily depends upon whether or not colleges are seriously recruiting him based upon his responses to the RDR Recruiting Assessment. The range of services that are available to you can vary by price and the service(s) you choose. I recommend a company that not only utilizes the internet and technology, but also one that takes the time to personally meet with you and your son throughout every step of his recruiting process. This ensures that the individual assisting you is able to accurately assess and gauge your son's true athletic ability; as well as, make any necessary adjustments to his current recruiting needs as they arise and as your son matures.

Factors to Consider Prior to Paying for Assistance

Despite being frowned upon for one reason or another, there are many competent and qualified recruiting professionals or services that can assist your son throughout his recruiting process and help him:

1. Develop an athletic resume (his player profile).
2. Develop an effective recruiting plan specific to his ability level.
3. Produce a quality, college ready DVD highlight film.
4. Learn all about the NCAA's current eligibility guidelines.
5. Avoid today's most common recruiting mistakes.
6. Accurately assess both his academic and athletic abilities.
7. Determine which level of college football is right for him and help him target the right schools.
8. Expose his talents on-line.

It bears repeating that grades and ability are paramount in the scholarship evaluation process, so *"NO ONE (SERVICE) CAN GUARANTEE YOUR SON A SCHOLARSHIP OR HAS AN ALL-INCLUSIVE FORMULA TO HELP HIM OBTAIN ONE."* Shop around, do your research, and find assistance that is competent and right for him. Factors to consider prior to seeking and paying for outside recruiting assistance include:

- The **COST(S)** of the service(s).
- Your abilities as a parent to assist your son (e.g., your writing ability, technological abilities, video production abilities).
- How much time do you have to devote to your son's recruiting efforts? Remember, marketing your son to schools is a year-round job that is time consuming and difficult.
- How involved are his coaches with helping him with his recruiting efforts?
- Does the recruiting source have experience working directly with athletes in the recruiting process (check their resume and the companies background)?

- Will the source actually sit down with you and your son and spend time with you?
- Do you and your son both trust and feel comfortable with the source?
- Does the source actually understand today's entire recruiting process, and all of the current NCAA guidelines?
- Is the source capable of developing a comprehensive recruiting plan specific to your son's abilities?
- Can the source teach you how to avoid the most common recruiting mistakes?

Online Recruiting Services

Recruiting services have capitalized on the 'boom' in technology and are now prevalent on the World Wide Web. A Google search today will identify a number of online recruiting services that vary in size and in services based upon your financial commitment. Many advertise themselves as a "do it all" recruiting solution that will help you market and expose your son to hundreds, if not thousands of colleges; as well as, sell the concept of how important online exposure is in helping your son obtain a scholarship. Typically, on-line recruiting services will allow your son to create a player profile, allow him to upload his highlight video(s), photos and/or his other pertinent football information onto their site for a specified period of time (typically one year) and for a specified fee.

Opponents of on-line services would argue that some are expensive (sometimes as much as $5,000), have no real personal contact with their clients, and do little, if anything, to actually help prospects gain exposure or receive scholarships. Not to mention, college coaches rarely, if ever, rely on them for recruiting information or prospect referrals. Despite these criticisms, there are plenty of free or inexpensive online recruiting services that are worthwhile and that can help your son gain exposure. Although the internet is a wonderful tool to help promote your son and his abilities, solely relying on this medium for exposure throughout his recruiting process is a mistake. Whatever option you decide, proceed with caution, do your research on any online recruiting services or any individual offering you or your son recruiting assistance.

If you are still undecided as to whether or not your son needs recruiting assistance after considering the above options, I recommend that you strongly consider outside recruiting help if he has no written offers, is not being seriously recruited, does not have a quality highlight film ready for college evaluation, or is in need of a recruiting plan. I also recommend that you pull out all of the stops in order to aggressively market him to colleges on a year-round basis, especially if your son has the grades and the ability to play college football. As you have already read, the competition for football scholarships is fierce and the odds of obtaining a full-scholarship are slim. If you procrastinate, do nothing to help promote your son or gain a recruiting advantage for him, then there are plenty of other parents out there that will promote their son and take your place. More importantly, you will never know if any of these options could have worked in your son's favor to help him gain exposure or obtain a scholarship.

The Role of Your Son's Head Coach

Let's take a moment to talk in detail about your son's head coach as he relates to his recruiting process. The head coach can undoubtedly be one of your son's biggest assets in this process and may have several college connections that could assist your son in his search for the right college and a scholarship. However, do not assume that the head coach knows everything about the recruiting process, has the time or the expertise to aggressively market your son. In reality, coaches have a lot going on in their lives besides your son, and few aggressively market all of their players in the same manner. Regardless, I recommend you and your son:

- Frequently ask for recruiting assistance from the head coach.
- Ask for his feedback and evaluation as to your son's ability level and which level of college football and/or schools to target.
- Ask him for copies of your son's game films.
- Ask if he can help you make a highlight film for your son or evaluate his existing film.
- Provide him with updated copies of his highlight film and player profile.

- Frequently consult him to find out if he has received any correspondence from colleges through his office and share with him any correspondence your son received at home.

There is much debate as to the role of a head coach as it relates to his players' college recruitment or lack thereof. Always respect your son's head coach and his position even if he is not your son's "go to" recruiting resource or he is not the one that helps him obtain a scholarship. Again, remember that *you are your son's greatest recruiting asset*.

Components 5 and 6: The Highlight Film and Marketing Your Son

In today's recruiting process, it is all about being proactive, utilizing technology, building relationships and marketing. In keeping pace with technology, the highlight film has today become the single most important recruiting "tool" in the recruiting process. Never undervalue or ignore the importance of a quality highlight film in your son's recruiting plan. Your son will not catch the eye of a coach, be evaluated by a recruiter, nor receive a football scholarship without having a quality highlight film formatted onto a DVD disc and supporting game film that accurately displays his talents and ability level.

Secondly, you must utilize technology and proactively market your son to colleges on a year-round basis; as well as, showcase his abilities via the internet, at combines, summer camps, and during visits to college campuses. If you are not doing this, then there are many other players just as talented as your son that will. Please read Chapter's 5 and 6 carefully since they detail the fifth and sixth components of your son's recruiting plan and there are numerous tips and strategies to assist you in the development of your son's highlight film; as well as, strategies on how to effectively market him to colleges.

Chapter 3
The Offer, the Verbal Commitment,
and
National Signing Day

"The difference between a prospect being 'LIKED' and 'LOVED' (by a college or university) is an 'OFFER."

Your son will begin his college recruiting journey as a *prospective student-athlete or prospect* the moment he starts ninth-grade classes. As his recruiting journey progresses and he begins to receive interest and contact from college coaches, and/or take official visits college campuses, he now officially becomes what is commonly known as a *recruit.* As a recruit, the ultimate goal is to receive written scholarship offers and sign a full scholarship. The *"offer"* (i.e., verbal offer- written offer- scholarship offer) is probably the most commonly used and repeated recruiting term you will hear throughout your son's recruiting process.

Today, unproven and undeveloped prospects both academically and athletically are receiving verbal scholarship offers the moment they enter high school. This disturbing trend of college coaches racing to secure early verbal commitments from young recruits at a feverous pace has led to what some now refer to as an 'arms-race' mentality to extending scholarship offers. Currently, football recruits are eligible to receive written scholarship offers on September 1 of their junior year. However, in April 2010, the NCAA passed legislation which changed this date to August 1 of a recruit's senior year for the class of 2012 and thereafter.

The offer process typically starts when a college coach verbally extends the scholarship offer to a targeted recruit. When permitted as noted above, the college or university will (should) then follow-up by fax or mail with the official *written offer* to the recruit's head coach. The written offer is not an actual scholarship, but rather a formal letter from the schools head football coach informing the recruit of the school's intent to officially extend him a full scholarship offer, congratulating him, and outlining all of the conditions that he must fulfill in order to receive an official scholarship on national signing day. Today, it is typical for a top-rated prospect (blue-chip prospect) to have multiple verbal and/or written offers prior to their senior season and national signing day.

The Verbal Commitment

Ideally, as your son progresses through his recruiting process and as he approaches his senior year, he should be eligible by NCAA standards, and narrowing his choice of scholarship offers. In fact, he may even know which school is right for him prior to national signing day. If this is the case, he can *verbally commit* to a school prior to national signing day. Today, it is not uncommon for a recruit to verbally commit early, either sometime during their junior year or during the football season of their senior year. Players usually do this after evaluating schools for months, visiting them, weighing each school's pros and cons, and after engaging in thorough discussions with family, friends and their coaches. Neither a written offer nor a player's subsequent verbal commitment is binding. However, with all things being fair, a recruits verbal commitment stands as a verbal promise to the coach and to the university that they will act in good faith for the remainder of the recruiting process and ultimately sign a *National Letter of Intent* (NLI)—the NCAA's official document that binds an athlete to the a college or university for one academic year. In turn, the school will honor their commitment of the scholarship offer. However, it is worth noting that a school will most likely withdraw a scholarship offer if a recruit falls into any sort of legal and/or academic trouble prior to national signing day and unfortunately in some instances, when they sustain an injury.

Despite a prospect's best intentions, considering the pressures associated with the recruiting process and a prospect's maturity level, it is not unusual for them to have a change of heart after verbally committing to a school, and *"de-commit"*. Although de-committing is legal, keep in mind that recruiting is a sensitive business and if this should occur, the school that your son is de-committing from may take this broken promise personally and decide to stop recruiting him altogether and rescind the verbal and/or written offer. On the other hand, the school may be understanding, really want to sign your son and continue recruiting him despite his change of heart. Regardless, prior to your son de-committing, make sure that he has other viable offers since many of his original offers might have been withdrawn upon his original verbal commitment. Due to the increasing number of prospects de-committing today, it has led to the emergence of a new term in the recruiting vernacular called the "*soft verbal*". A recruit who designates himself as a soft verbal to a particular school is essentially declaring that although he will verbally commit early to a school, he will also keep his options open, consider other schools and officially visit those schools at some point during his recruiting process.

Criteria for Selecting a College

I also recommend that your son **not** make any commitment decision until both you and he visit his school of choice, you have thoroughly researched the school and discussed the pros and cons pertaining to the important *criteria for selecting a school*. Criteria for choosing a school include:

- Its location.
- The school's academic reputation, accreditation, various degree programs and the player graduation rates.
- Its level of competition and is it a good choice for your son?
- The stability of the coaching staff and the school's athletic department.
- Your son's comfort level—does it feel like "home" and does he truly "love" the school?
- The depth of players currently on the roster in your son's position. Will he play right away?
- What position is the school recruiting him to play at?
- The campuses social environment.
- Whether it is a school your son would attend even if he did not play football.
- Athletic facilities.

Once your son has decided to verbally commit, he should call his recruiter and the school's head coach in order to notify them of his verbal commitment. If he honors his verbal commitment to the school and he is not going to consider other offers (*'strong verbal)*, then he should call all of the other schools that have offered him and those that he is seriously considering in order to update them on his verbal commitment and thank them for their time and offers. This cordial gesture will allow these schools an opportunity to move forward with their respective recruiting efforts.

National Signing Day and the National Letter of Intent (NLI)

Now that your son is firmly committed and his decision is final, we move forward to national signing day. The joy of national signing day is like no other for a student-athlete as their family, fellow teammates, and coaches gather to celebrate the achievement of moving to the next level. The day is complete with tears of joy, smiles, and a steady stream of well-wishers. You will feel a tremendous sense of pride and satisfaction knowing that your and your son's years of hard work and sacrifice have finally paid off, he now has the opportunity to play college football, and more importantly receive a college education. Oh, I almost forgot—you are also at peace knowing the financial burden of paying for college has been lifted off your shoulders!

Each year, the NCAA designates the first Wednesday in February as national signing day for high school football recruits. As noted above, it is the most memorable day of your son's high school football career; as well as, the culminating day in your son's recruiting process. On national signing day, the parent (or legal guardian) and the athlete; as well as, the college or university's athletic director will sign a National Letter of Intent (NLI). The NLI is the NCAA's official document that binds a student-athlete to the college or university of their choice for one academic year providing they are officially admitted to the institution and eligible under NCAA rules. The NLI stipulates specific penalties if the athlete does not follow through on his/her signed commitment, such as losing a year of eligibility if they back out or transfer to another school after signing. In addition, the NLI specifies that the athlete intends to enroll at the institution in the fall, outlines the type and extent of financial aid the institution will be providing, and requires that other institutions accept the athlete's decision as final and agree not to recruit them any further. There are specific NLI dates for each sport and they change slightly with each calendar year. For more information as to the official first and last day a recruit can sign an NLI so visit http://www.national-letter.org to learn more about the NCAA's current NLI signing dates and regulations.

Chapter 4

Academics and NCAA Eligibility

"It is not the mountain we conquer but ourselves."

Sir Edmund Hillary

WARNING: Your son's senior year is not the time for him to start boosting his grade point average (GPA) in hopes that he will qualifying for a scholarship, nor is it the time for him to lose a scholarship because his grades slip, he fails a required core class, or fails to achieve a passing score on the SAT or ACT exam.

Being a serious minded student-athlete dedicated to obtaining an athletic scholarship starts as early as middle school. As it relates to academics, obtaining a scholarship is a marathon, not a sprint. Therefore, in order to avoid the disastrous scenario outlined above, have your son make a note of these important **academic tips** during his recruiting process:

1. The earlier your son becomes a qualifier, the better his chances are for an athletic scholarship.
2. The higher his core GPA is, the better his chances are for a scholarship.
3. Be consistent—being a qualifier one month does not guarantee that your son will be a qualifier at a future time if his core GPA and/or grades decline.
4. Strive for and achieve greatness both on and off the field—college coaches today are looking for a complete student-athlete who is a well-rounded individual.
5. Never assume your son's athletic prowess will trump his academic ability.

6. Tell your son to push himself academically throughout high school and until his last final exam is complete.

So what is a realistic academic bar and eligibility threshold to set for your son throughout high school in order to ensure that he qualifies for an athletic scholarship? Again, as an educator, my answer is simple: set the bar high in order to allow for some wiggle room in case he hits a rough stretch during high school.

> **ACADEMIC TIP**: Ensure your son maintains at least a 3.0 core GPA throughout high school and achieves at least an 860 on the SAT exam, or combined ACT score of at least 75, which is a 'composite score' of 19 (75 divided by the four (4) test sections—then round to the nearest whole number).

If this academic threshold seems unrealistic for your son's ability, **PREPARE** at the beginning of his freshman year to seek academic assistance or make an investment in assistance such as subject specific tutoring. Whether he is above or below these marks, continuously monitor his core GPA in correlation to the NCAA's sliding scale *(see Appendices C and D)*. Maintaining a high academic standard will ensure that your son stays eligible throughout high school and realistically qualifies for an athletic scholarship. With outstanding grades and test scores, he may even qualify for an academic scholarship. Also remember that eligibility requirements at the other football division levels and the NAIA level are completely different from Division I eligibility requirements.

The National Collegiate Athletic Association (NCAA)

The NCAA is a non-profit organization of about twelve hundred colleges, universities and athletic conferences, and is responsible for governing all aspects of intercollegiate athletics; as well as, enforcing all NCAA rules. The NCAA's Web site (www.ncaa.org) is a good reference point for parents and athletes alike, as it details all of the rules and regulations regarding recruiting practices, provides recruits with information to help them know their rights, and most importantly, outlines all eligibility standards. Throughout this chapter, we will detail the NCAA's eligibility requirements; as well as, other pertinent eligibility standards you and your son must know throughout his recruiting process.

The recommended starting point for all high school freshman athletes who wish to pursue college athletics is to read and become familiar with the NCAA's *Guide for the College Bound Student Athlete*. This free, easy-to-read publication summarizes all of the pertinent rules and regulations, such as guidelines related to recruiting, eligibility, financial aid and the initial college freshman eligibility requirements for Divisions I- and II-bound athletes. The guide can be downloaded directly from the NCAA's Web site, or you can call to order it at 1-800-638-3731.

What is an NCAA Qualifier?

In order for a high school football player to officially become eligible to play at the NCAA level (Division I and II), and be considered a *'qualifier'*, they must meet all of the criteria outlined below.

Table 3 *NCAA Eligibility Requirements for Divisions I- and II- Football*

		Division I	Division II
1.	Graduate from high school	required	required
2.	Number of required core courses	16	14
3.	Required core-course grade point average (Core GPA) (See Appendices C and D)	Earn a Core GPA that matches your test score based upon the sliding scale	Minimum 2.000 Core GPA
4.	Qualifying test score (See Appendices C and D)	Earn a combined SAT or ACT sum score that matches your Core GPA based upon the sliding scale	Minimum SAT score of 820 or ACT sum score of 68
5.	Complete the clearinghouse registration process at www.ncaaclearinghouse.net	required	required
6.	Complete the amateurism questionnaire and request a final amateurism certification.	required	required

Assuming that your son will meet the NCAA's first criteria for eligibility (high school graduation) let us discuss the NCAA's *second* criteria for eligibility, or an athlete's required core course completion.

The NCAA's official core course requirements for Division I and II football are outlined below.

Table 4 *NCAA Core Courses Requirements for Division I- and II- Football*

Division I (16 Core Courses)	Division II (14 Core Courses)
4 years of English	3 years of English
3 years of Mathematics (Algebra 1 or higher)	2 years of Mathematics (Algebra 1 or higher)
2 years of Natural/Physical Science (1 year of lab)	2 years of Natural/Physical Science (1 year of lab)
1 year of additional English, Mathematics, or Natural/Physical Science	2 years of additional English, Mathematics, or Natural/Physical Science.
2 years of Social Science	2 years of Social Science
4 years of additional courses (from any area above or a foreign language, non-doctrinal Religion/Philosophy, Computer Science)	3 years of additional courses (from any area above or a foreign language, non- doctrinal Religion/Philosophy)

** Beginning 2013, Division II athletes will be required to complete sixteen core courses.

Your son's guidance counselor should be able to provide you with the school's list of NCAA-approved core courses that your son is required to take for each academic year. If you would like to find them yourself, follow these steps:

1. Go to the NCAA Eligibility Center Web site at www.ncaaclearinghouse.net and login.
2. Click on "General Information."
3. Click on "List of Approved Core Courses."
4. Input the high school's CEEB code (if you know it, or search by the high school's name and state).
5. Review the list.

If you do not find your son's list of NCAA-approved core courses on the Eligibility Center's Web site, you can call the NCAA directly at (877) 262-1492.

WARNING: Core courses that appear on your son's transcript must exactly match the courses specified on his schools list of NCAA-approved core courses. Any core course not on this list will not be used for eligibility determination.

Immediately consult his guidance counselor if you discover that your son has taken a course that is not on his school's official core course list. A designated individual at your son's high school is responsible for keeping this list updated to ensure that the core courses athletes are taking appear on the school's official list.

> **ACADEMIC TIP:** You and your son must meet regularly with a qualified guidance counselor to make sure that the courses he is taking or has taken exactly match his school's list of NCAA approved core courses (see the RPP in Appendices F- I).

Important Core Course Facts

Some important facts regarding core course work as it relates to the NCAA's guidelines include:

- Student-athletes must utilize their high school's policy regarding the lowest acceptable passing grade for a course. If the Eligibility Center does not have this policy, the lowest passing grade that will be used is a D.

- The NCAA **does not accept** credit-by-exam courses.

- The NCAA **does not accept** vocational courses (e.g., typing, auto mechanics, driver's education, and health).

- Pass/Fail grades **may** satisfy core course requirements. However, the NCAA's Eligibility Center will assign the high school's lowest passing grade for a pass/fail class.

- Courses taken in the eighth grade that are high school core courses (e.g., Algebra I, Spanish 1, Freshman Composition) **may** be used to meet the core course requirement if the course is on the student-athletes high school transcript with a grade and credit and if the course is on the high school's NCAA list of approved core courses.

Independent-study, Internet (online), and correspondence courses **count** as core courses as long as the following conditions are met:

1. The course meets core course requirements.

2. The student and the instructor had 'on-going access' to each other during the course so that the instructor was able to teach, evaluate, and assist them.

3. The student's work (for example, exams, papers, assignments) is available for review and validation.

4. The high school or secondary school program identifies a defined time for completion of the course.

5. Appropriate academic authorities evaluated each student's work according to the high school's academic policies.

6. The course was acceptable for any student to take and the course was placed on the student's high school transcript.

Since the NCAA has recently begun to crack down on athletes cheating in these courses and on certain online course providers that do not meet the criteria outlined above, *ensure that the NCAA accepts the course and the online course provider prior to your son registering for the online course.*

College courses may be used to satisfy core curriculum requirements as well if the courses are accepted and awarded credit by the high school for any student and meet all other requirements for core courses. For NCAA Division I only, such courses must be placed on the student's high school transcript. Courses taken at a college will **NOT** appear on the high school's NCAA list of approved core courses since only courses offered and taught by the high school will appear on an NCAA list of approved core courses. In addition, a one-year course that is spread over a longer period of time is considered **one** course and will receive a maximum of **one** core course credit (example: Algebra 1, spread over two years, would receive one unit of credit).

If a student-athlete attended a secondary school outside the United States for all or part of grades nine through twelve, different evaluation procedures will be applied to their international education documents. The student must submit original-language documents with certified translations for Eligibility Center evaluation. Also, as it relates to incoming Division I athletes:

- Only courses completed in grades nine through twelve will qualify as core courses.

- Student's **may use one** core course completed in the year after graduation (summer or academic year), providing they graduated from high school on schedule (in eight semesters). They **may** complete the core course at a location other than the high school from which they graduated and **may** initially enroll full time at a collegiate institution at any time after completion of the core course.

- Students with *diagnosed disabilities* (if it has been properly diagnosed and documented), **may** use one or more core courses completed after high school but before full-time enrollment in college.

- Students with appropriately *diagnosed education-impacted disabilities* **may** use courses for students with education-impacted disabilities for meeting NCAA core course requirements. However, courses for students with education-impacted disabilities must appear on the high school's NCAA list of approved core courses in order for a student to receive NCAA credit for the course.

- Finally, if a student attended more than one high school during their career, they must provide the NCAA with official transcripts from *each* school where they completed a core course.

On the other hand, for Division II core course requirements, all core courses completed before a student's full-time enrollment at any college may be used by the Eligibility Center.

How to Calculate and Monitor Your Son's Core GPA

The NCAA's *third* and *fourth* criteria for eligibility are based upon an athlete achieving a qualifying core-course grade point average (core GPA) relevant to a qualifying (or matching) SAT or ACT score based upon the NCAA's sliding scale (Appendices C and D). An athlete's core course GPA is simply the average of their best grades achieved for all required core courses. As noted earlier, the Division II and the NAIA football eligibility requirements are completely different from Division I, but the major difference is that there is no sliding scale requirement. For athletes desiring to play Division II football, the minimum core grade point average for eligibility purposes is a 2.000 along with a minimum SAT score of 820 (verbal and math sections only) and/or a minimum combined ACT score of 68.

If an athlete has taken extra core courses, those courses will be used in their GPA calculation only if they improve their GPA. In addition, a school's normal practice of weighting honors or advanced courses may be used, as long as the weighting is used for computing GPAs. Weighting cannot be used if the high school weights grades for the purpose of determining class rank. Additionally, in no instance may the student receive greater than one additional quality point for purposes of calculating the GPA for initial eligibility. On the next page, is an example of how to calculate your son's core GPA.

Example: Your son completed three (3) core courses during an academic year and each class is worth one credit. The quality point value for each grade is as follows: A=4, B=3, C=2 and a D=1.

Course Title	Credits X	Grade =	Quality Points
1. English 1	1	B	(1 X 3) = 3
2. Algebra 1	1	C	(1 X 2) = 2
3. Biology	1	A	(1 X 4) = 4
Total Credits= 3			Total: 9

Total Quality Points		Total Credits	Cumulative Core GPA
9	**÷**	**3**	**3.000**

To become eligible for a Division I football scholarship with a 3.000 core GPA, your son will be required to obtain a minimum SAT score (see sliding scale Appendix C) of 620 and/or a 'combined' ACT score of 52. Which is also an ACT '*composite* (average) *score*' of 13 (52 divided by 4).

On the other hand, if your son has a much lower core GPA, let's say a 2.100, then he must obtain a much higher SAT test score of 970 and/or a combined ACT score of 82—which is a composite score of 21 (82 divided by 4) to become eligible. For your convenience, this guide includes a GPA log (see Appendices A and B) so that you can continuously monitor, track, and calculate your son's current core GPA.

Registering for the NCAA's Clearinghouse

The NCAA's *fifth* eligibility criterion pertains to registering with the NCAA's Clearinghouse. If a student-athlete intends to participate in Division I or II athletics as a freshman, they must register and submit their official core class high school transcripts and standardized test scores (ACT or SAT) **directly** to the NCAA Clearinghouse. However, if an athlete intends to participate at the

Division III or NAIA levels, they are not required to register for the Clearinghouse.

ACADEMIC TIP: The NCAA recommends that your son register with the Clearinghouse at the beginning of his junior year, in case he must address any academic deficiencies during his senior year.

Student-athletes can register for the NCAA Clearinghouse online at (www.ncaaclearinghouse.net), or call (877) 262-1492 for registration materials. Upon completing Clearinghouse registration, they will receive an official ten-digit Clearinghouse registration number. This official number identifies the student-athlete within the NCAA's Clearinghouse database in case they need to submit future academic information to the Clearinghouse. Registering for the Clearinghouse is simple, inexpensive and is **required prior to your son taking any 'official' visit to a college campus**.

The Importance of a Transcript Credit-Analysis

Throughout high school, it is vital that you constantly monitor your son's academic progress and do everything you possibly can to ensure that he stays academically focused. It is recommended that you and he meet at least twice a year (beginning in his freshman year) with his guidance counselor in order to complete what is known a "*transcript credit analysis*." A transcript credit analysis is a comprehensive review of your son's official high school transcript by a qualified guidance counselor. His *official transcript* is the certified school document that lists all of the high school courses your son has taken and the grades received for each course; as well as, his current weighted and un-weighted grade point averages. In addition, this official document ***must be sent directly*** to both the NCAA's Clearinghouse and any selected college or university admission office upon request. A comprehensive transcript credit analysis will determine:

1. If your son is (or is not) on track to graduate on time in eight academic semesters or earlier.

2. How many credits your son has accumulated and how many more credits he will need to graduate.

3. Your son's current core grade point average (GPA), and his current weighted and un-weighted GPA (always know both).

4. If your son's core courses meet NCAA eligibility requirements.

Keep in mind that when a college recruiter is seriously evaluating your son, at some point they will request a copy of his official transcript in order to conduct the same type of assessment, evaluate his academic potential and check his current academic standing. Therefore, always know where your son stands academically and *never conceal or hold back his academic information or his transcript from a college coach if this document is requested.*

ACADEMIC TIP: Always maintain a file with copies of your son's current transcript and copies of his latest ACT/SAT test scores in the event that a college coach requests these important documents for review—whether or not your son is in good academic standing or is already qualified.

Weighted vs. Un-Weighted GPA

Since you have heard the terms weighted and un-weighted GPA mentioned above in relation to your son's official transcript, and your son, his guidance counselor or other school personnel may refer to these important academic terms during your transcript discussions, it is vital for you to understand the difference between the two terms and know how to calculate each one.

Quite simply, a *weighted* GPA allows for honors, Advanced Placement (AP), and International Baccalaureate (IB) courses that your son takes to count for one extra grade point. For example:

The quality point value for a student that receives a letter grade of an 'A' in a weighted AP English course is equal to 5.0 quality points. Weighted Quality Point Values are as follows: 5=A, 4=B, 3=C, 2=D, 0=F

On the other hand, if a student received the same grade in a regular un-weighted English course, then the 'A' is equal to 4.0 quality points. Un-weighted Quality Point Values are as follows: 4=A, 3=B, 2=C, 1=D, 0=F

Having identified the two different quality point values, let us move on to an actual example that calculates both a weighted and an un-weighted GPA utilizing a standard GPA calculation formula—(Total number of quality points ÷ Total number of classes = GPA).

Example 1: A student receives an 'A', a 'B', and a 'C' as their final grades. The class they received the 'A' in was a weighted Advanced Placement (AP) class. Their weighted GPA calculation would be as follows:

$$\boxed{5}+3+2 \div 3 = 3.33 \; weighted \; GPA$$

Example 2: A student receives the exact final grades of an 'A', a 'B', and a 'C'. However, the class in which they received the 'A' in was an un-weighted class. Their un-weighted GPA calculation would be as follows:

$$\boxed{4}+3+2 \div 3 = 3.00 \; un\text{-}weighted \; GPA$$

Since a weighted GPA allows a class to count for more points, your son's weighted GPA will always be higher than his un-weighted GPA.

Today, most high schools have a guidance counselor who is familiar with the NCAA's eligibility requirements specifically related to athletics. These counselors are able to assist coaches, parents and athletes in finding the answers to important eligibility questions, accurately calculating player grade point averages and tracking an athlete's academic progress to ensure that they meet NCAA eligibility standards. Therefore, it is important for you to identify who this counselor is at your son's school early on so they can assist you.

> **ACADEMIC TIP:** <u>Always</u> have an academic plan to assist your son and to assure college coaches that he will correct any academic deficiencies and meet NCAA eligibility standards.

About the ACT and SAT Exams

In your son's sophomore year, he can prepare for and take the Preliminary SAT (PSAT) exam. The PSAT is a great practice test for the SAT, and if he receives a high score on the exam, he could qualify for a National Merit Scholarship. Your son should finalize his SAT (also known as the SAT Reasoning Test) or ACT (also known as the American College Testing exam) preparation in the summer prior to his Junior year, and be prepared to take either exam as early as October of that same year. The sooner he takes either exam (or both if he prefers) and obtains a qualifying score, the sooner he can become eligible, and the better his chances are for a scholarship or an offer. Remember, based on the NCAA's sliding scale in Appendices C and D, the higher your son's core GPA, the lower his qualifying ACT/SAT exam score needs to be, but the lower his core GPA is, the higher his qualifying test score will need to be.

> **NCAA REQUIREMENT** – All prospective Division I and II athletes <u>must</u> have their ACT/SAT exam scores <u>sent directly</u> to the NCAA's Clearinghouse from the testing agencies. Exam scores posted on a student-athletes transcript are no longer valid for test verification. To send exam scores directly to the NCAA, use the Eligibility Centers code of <u>**9999**</u> as a score recipient upon registering for either exam.

Which exam your son takes to qualify primarily depends on his comfort level, his preparation and his academic background, but keep in mind that these are two different tests. Table 5 on the next page highlights the differences between the two exams in both structure and in format.

Table 5 *ACT vs. SAT Structure and Format*

	ACT	SAT
Length	3 hours 25 min (with Writing Test)	3 hours 45 minutes
Structure	4 Sections (English, Math, Reading, Science) plus an optional Writing Test	10 Sections (3 Critical Reading, 3 Math, 3 Writing, and 1 Experimental, which is un-scored)
Wrong Answer Penalty	No penalty for wrong answers	¼ point subtracted from your Raw Score for each wrong answer (except for Math Grid-Ins)
Reading	Reading Comprehension	Reading Comprehension Sentence Completions
Math	Arithmetic, Algebra, Geometry Algebra II, Trigonometry	Arithmetic, Algebra, Geometry Algebra II
Science	Analysis, Interpretation, Evaluation, Basic Content Problem Solving	Not applicable
Essay	Optional final section 30 minutes Not Included in Composite Score Topic of importance to high school students	First section, 25 minutes Factored into overall score More abstract topic

One of the most notable differences between the two exams is in their scoring. The SAT exam score is based upon the verbal and math sections only, and the writing section is not applicable. On the other hand, the ACT score is based upon four test section scores: English, Math, Reading, Science or Combined English/Writing. The ACT also averages the combined score to create a *'composite (average) score'* that is rounded to the nearest whole number. Some athletes take both the ACT and SAT exams; some take one or the other to achieve a qualifying score and some take both more than once, even after achieving a qualifying score on both. In addition, students with diagnosed education-impacted disabilities may take a nonstandard ACT or SAT exam.

Regardless as to which exam your son decides to take, consult with his guidance counselor to find out if his school offers free exam tutoring, study materials or a prep course (during or after school) prior to taking the exam or spending any money on an expensive tutoring prep course. To be safe, push to have your son academically eligible as early as possible, but no later than the spring of his junior year. In the 'Web sites' section, you will find the home pages for both testing Web sites so that you may obtain the current testing dates for each exam, registration requirements and exam costs.

Early Graduation

A popular option these days for high school football players is to graduate early in December of their senior year, and *'green shirt'*, or enroll early in their selected college or university in January for the spring semester and to participate in spring football practice. If your son desires to go this route, there are several factors to consider. First and foremost, you should sit down with him to determine if he is in fact "mature" enough both mentally and physically to handle this rapid transition. Keep in mind that your son is pushing up his graduation date by almost six months, and his preparation time required to qualify academically is significantly reduced. Secondly, you will have to meet with his guidance counselor, early on in his junior year to map out an accelerated graduation exit plan specifically for him that adheres to all state and local school district graduation requirements.

Once you have decided that this option is right for him and your plan is in place, you must closely monitor and track your son's academic progress. He, in turn, must discipline himself to stay on track by meeting all of his academic requirements, maintain his accelerated graduation pace, and complete the required course work (or exams) at the specified times since there is no margin for error. Your son will be required to take additional course loads during the summer time and may be required to take classes simultaneously during the day and in the evening for an extended period of time in order to meet all graduation requirements. Most school districts have options to take extra courses to improve a student's GPA, or to graduate early in programs such as summer school, adult evening classes, and online high school completion courses. So again, consult his guidance counselor to find out all of his available options.

Types of Athletic Scholarships and Other Financial Assistance

Based upon guidelines, the NCAA classifies athletic scholarships as either *partial* or *full* and each type of scholarship has set parameters that are mandated by the NCAA.

1. A full athletic scholarship (full grant-in-aid or full ride) will pay for the full amount of an athlete's tuition, university fees, required textbooks, and room and board. Most Division I (FBS) level football players are awarded full football scholarships since the NCAA stipulates that any student receiving a partial scholarship at the Division I level counts fully against the total allotment of eighty-five scholarships (The NCAA, "Recruiting Definitions", 2010).

2. Unlike a full athletic scholarship, a partial athletic scholarship will only cover specific portions of an athlete's tuition, university fees, textbooks, and/or room and board expenses. Since football scholarships are limited at the FCS level (I-AA) and Division II levels, it is common for theses institutions to split scholarships between athletes and only award partial scholarships.

What is a Walk-On?

If your son does not receive a scholarship or any form of athletic aid, but still chooses to play college football, he can choose to "*walk on*" to make the team. As a walk-on athlete, he must be admitted to his chosen college or university based upon the same standards as any other student applying to the college. The admissions department will not grant him any special admission consideration because of his athletic intentions. Depending upon your son's performance during the season, both athletically and academically, the coaching staff may offer him a partial or full scholarship in a subsequent season.

Need-Based Financial Aid

In the event that your son requires student financial aid to assist him with college, he may be eligible to receive non-athletic funding to help pay for his educational expenses including tuition, fees, room and board, and/or books and supplies. Financial aid is not a loan. In order to qualify for federal, state, and institutional aid a student must first prepare a *Free Application for Federal Student Aid* (FAFSA) each year and aid is awarded based on the financial need of the student.

The FAFSA is approximately 130 questions, considers household size, income, assets, the number family members in college, and other financial factors to determine a student's aid eligibility and what is known as the *expected family contribution* or (EFC). College institutions use the EFC to guide their decision about how much need-based financial aid to award a student.

> **FINANCIAL AID TIP:** Financial aid is distributed on a first-come, first-served basis. If your son is in jeopardy of not receiving an athletic scholarship or any type of athletic financial assistance, it is crucial that he prepare and submit his FASFA application as close to January 1 as possible during his senior year.

At a private institution, a supplemental application may be necessary for institutional need-based aid.

You may prepare your FAFSA federal student aid application either online at the U.S. Department of Education's Web site (www.fafsa.ed.gov) or by using the services of a fee-based, professional aid advisory firm. The table below details the most common types of federal financial aid grant options available. The United States government and all U.S. state governments provide some type of merit and need-based student aid including grants, work-study programs, and loans. The (EFC) also takes into consideration any participation in college savings or pre-paid tuition plans. In the past, financial aid officers weighed pre-paid tuition plans more heavily than other 529 College Savings Plans (see glossary of terms) when determining a student's eligibility. However, in February 2006, Congress passed legislation to treat both types of plans evenly.

Table 6 *Different Types of Financial Aid (Quick Reference Guide)*

Program	Type of Aid	Program Details	Annual Award Amount
Federal Pell Grant	Does not have to be repaid	Available to undergraduates; all eligible students will receive the Federal Pell Grant amounts they qualify for	$400 to $5,350
Federal Supplemental Educational Opportunity Grant (FSEOG)	Does not have to be repaid	For undergraduates with exceptional financial need; priority is given to Federal Pell Grant recipients; funds depend on availability at school	$500 to $4,000
Federal Work-Study	Money is earned while attending school; does not have to be repaid	For undergraduate and graduate students; jobs can be on campus or off campus; students are paid at least minimum wage	No annual minimum or maximum award amounts
Academic Competitiveness Grant (ACG Grant)	Does not have to be repaid	Grant is awarded in addition to the Federal Pell Grant	$750 for the first year of study and up to $1,300 for the second year

Most state governments typically provide some form of need- and non-need-based aid, consisting of grants, loans, work-study programs, tuition waivers, and/or scholarships. Individual colleges and universities offer similar options as well. Some institutions may require only the FAFSA and others may require additional need-based analysis documents such as the College Scholarship Service (CSS)/Financial Aid Profile or (CSS) Profile, to apply for such funds because these forms apply a more stringent need analysis for awarding institutional funds. The *Federal Student Aid Information Center* can help you or your son complete the application process and provides free information about all federal student aid programs. You can call 1-800-4-FED-AID to speak to a specialist about various student aid programs, or visit their Web site at http://federalstudentaid.ed.gov for current federal student aid information and resources.

Merit Based Scholarships (Academic)

In addition to need-based financial assistance, your son may qualify for and be awarded a merit-based (academic) scholarship from his selected college or an outside organization. Merit-based scholarships are awarded for outstanding high school academic achievements combined with minimum SAT or ACT scores, although some merit scholarships can be awarded for special talents, leadership potential and other personal characteristics. Scholarships may also be available via group affiliation such as the YMCA or the Boys Club. The advantage of a merit-based scholarship is that many recipients receive monies without regard for the financial need of the applicant. The other primary advantage of these scholarships is that you do not have to repay them as long as all of the scholarship requirements are met. At many colleges, every admitted student is automatically considered for their available merit scholarships. On the other hand, other schools require students to go through a separate application process for award consideration. Athletic scholarships are a form of merit aid that considers athletic talent.

Student Loans

Students requiring money beyond financial aid may have to consider an education loan. Typically, education loans obtained through the federal government have lower interest rates than private education loans. Below are examples of some college loan options. The Direct Loan Program includes Stafford and PLUS loans and is run by the U.S. Department of Education. Loan options include:

- Federal Stafford Loans: Federal Stafford loans are fixed-rate student loans for undergraduate and graduate students attending college at least half-time (6 credits). Stafford loans are one of the most reasonable (and most common) loan options to help pay for educational expenses. There are two loan options:

  - A *subsidized* Stafford loan offers a low fixed interest rate and the option of deferment (no payments) while enrolled in school. Acceptance is not based on credit.

- An *un-subsidized* Stafford loan offers increased borrowing amounts up to $2,000 more than subsidized loans, a fixed interest rate, and the option of deferment (no payments) while enrolled in school.

- State Student Incentive Grants and Federal PLUS Loans (http://www.parentplusloan.com) are loans borrowed by a parent on behalf of a child to help pay for tuition and school related expenses at an eligible college or university, or by a graduate student for graduate school. The student must be enrolled at least half time, and the parent or graduate student must pass a credit check in order to receive this loan.

- Federal Perkins Loans: This need-based loan program provides low-interest loans. Federal Perkins loans share many of the characteristics of subsidized Stafford loans such as no fees and a longer grace period. *Borrower's of these loans who go on to careers in public, military, or teaching service employment may be eligible to have all or part of their loans canceled.*

Appendix K further outlines various student loan options and you can learn more details about each specific loan by visiting the Stafford loan Web site at http://www.staffordloan.com. For current information on any of the loans listed above, visit the U.S. Department of Education's Direct Loan Web site for current loan information and loan requirements:

http://www2.ed.gov/offices/OSFAP/DirectLoan/index.html

Chapter 5
The Importance of a Quality Highlight Film

"You never get a second chance to make a first impression."

In addition to not having a recruiting plan, many recruits and parents underestimate and ignore the importance of a quality highlight film in the recruiting process. Your son's highlight film is without a doubt the single most important recruiting "tool" in his recruiting plan and is the key instrument that college coaches utilize today in order to evaluate athletes.

> Your son will not catch the eye of a college recruiter, will not be evaluated and not receive a football scholarship without having a quality highlight film (formatted onto a DVD disc) and supporting game film that accurately displays his talents and ability level.

Do not be fooled into believing that you can simply upload your son's highlight film onto YouTube or a single recruiting Web site and he will be discovered and receive a scholarship. Although I strongly support prospects marketing themselves online, over-reliance on these mediums is a mistake and can create a false sense of security. However, this is only one type of recruiting exposure and should only constitute one part of your son's recruiting plan. Currently, a highlight film posted on-line does not replace an actual DVD disc or game film directly in the hands of a college recruiter for evaluation. Only with an actual player's highlight film and/or game film in hand can a college coach and his entire staff collectively sit down and completely evaluate a prospect's potential; as well as, decide whether the school wants to pursue the prospect further. A prospect should always have an up-to-date highlight DVD that is ready to hand out to college recruiters or the recruiting media. Being prepared could help them get recognized, make a recruiting connection, and/or receive a scholarship offer. Simply put, without a quality highlight film in-hand, your son's recruiting process is like a ship adrift in the ocean without a destination.

The most common *highlight film mistakes* that prospects make in relation to the recruiting process include:

1. Not developing a highlight film or developing one too late.
2. Not having a quality highlight film suitable for a college recruiter's evaluation.
3. Having someone develop the highlight film who has **NO** experience in the recruiting process or in developing a football highlight film.
4. Not seeking feedback or evaluation from their coach(s) or a competent source prior to sending the highlight film to colleges.
5. Not sending their film to compatible schools.
6. Ignoring a college coach's request to send a highlight film for evaluation.
7. Only placing their highlight film on an online medium such as YouTube and not having an actual DVD disc on-hand.

When to Develop Your Son's Highlight Film

Unfortunately, many of the prospects that I encounter have no game film footage, cannot obtain their game film, and/or simply wait too long to put their highlight film together.

> **RECRUITING TIP:** By the time your son concludes his junior year at the varsity level, he should have a polished highlight film that includes at least three to four minutes of his best plays.

As outlined in our RPP (Appendix F), I encourage the development of a prospect's highlight film beginning in their freshman year and recommend updating the film from game-to-game until a polished product is available to send to college coaches for evaluation. Since the prospect monitoring and evaluation process is now beginning at the middle school level, why wait? Especially since college recruiters and the recruiting media are always on the lookout for the next wave of formidable prospects.

Key Components of a Highlight Film

Having quality game footage is the vital first step to producing a quality highlight film. Specifically, the game footage should be on a DVD disc, crystal clear, not blurred, and shaky or distorted in any way. In fact, the picture quality should be clear enough that each player and their jersey number are visible on the field. Since packaging and presentation are just as important as the film's content, ensure that you or the professional you hire utilize the latest video editing software to prepare the highlight film. Also, ensure that your son's best play's are at the beginning of the film. Key components of a highlight film include:

- Quality game footage on a DVD disc.
- Titles at the opening sequence of a film with your son's vital information, including his name, the name of his high school, his place of residence, position, jersey number and his year of graduation.
- His statistics, accomplishments, awards, his 40-yard dash time, his home/cell numbers, and his e-mail address.
- A length of no more than three to four minutes in duration.
- Proper ordering and sequencing of each highlight clip. Make sure the best highlight plays are at the beginning of the film.
- Special effects such as spot shadows, arrows and text that accentuate his best plays and ability.
- **NO** unnecessary graphics or effects such as rewind and slow motion, unnecessary content, or music (especially explicit music).

Continuously update the film after each game and subsequent season.

Producing a Film: Do-it-Yourself vs. Hiring a Professional

Going the do-it-yourself route and filming and/or producing your son's highlight film may prove to be a difficult task, but it is not an impossible one. As a parent who has been through this process and as a producer of player highlight films, I can personally tell you that it requires a substantial investment in time, in the right video camera and equipment, additional video supplies such as blank DVD's and in a good video-editing program. You will also be required to film each of your son's games or football related events, upload each film segment, and watch countless hours of video footage in order to select, edit and organize the right highlight clips to produce a polished product worthy of sending out to a college for evaluation. Ultimately, the quality of your finished product will depend upon the quality of your video camera, filming ability, computer savvy, time management, video-editing software and how well you utilize technology.

Ideally, you can save time and money if your son's head coach can provide you with his game film and produce his highlight film. However, keep in mind that the head coach may be extremely busy and obtaining his assistance may take some time, effort and persistence on your behalf. Another option to consider is asking a friend or fellow parent on the team for assistance, or hiring an experienced student who is involved in the audio/visual program at your son's school who would be willing to assist you for a small fee. Like most goods or services you purchase, you get what you pay for so be careful, especially when you are relying on a busy head coach or someone who has promised you that they would help you for free. When it comes to a highlight film, saving money should not be a priority when deciding who will produce your son's film. On the other hand, experience of the source producing the film, production quality and turn-around time should be a priority. If your son has to wait a considerable amount of time for his film while recruiter's are requesting copies of the film for evaluation, he may lose valuable opportunities to make recruiting connections and even an opportunity for a scholarship.

> **WARNING** – Never ignore a request from a college recruiter for a copy of your son's highlight film for evaluation.

If you choose to produce the highlight film yourself, your must decide whether or not to purchase a reliable hand held video camera or borrow one from a friend or relative. Secondly, utilize every opportunity to build your son's highlight collection by filming his games, his practice scrimmages and any off-season events such as a combine, a camp, or a 7-on-7 contest.

Five Key Video Camera Features

There are *five key features* to consider when purchasing your camera:

1. Format: Video formats include recording directly to DVD, recording in HD, or recording to a hard drive (recommended).

2. Optical vs. Digital Zoom: Both zoom types enlarge images for close-up recordings. Optical zoom capability uses the lens to enlarge without compromising image quality. Digital zoom essentially magnifies images, resulting in some loss of resolution.

3. Ease of Use: Do you like tinkering with lots of settings, or are you more of a point-and-shoot type? Who will be using your camcorder? What camcorder features are important to you?

4. Can the Camera Shoot Still Photos?: Most digital camcorders let you shoot still photos, but the higher the megapixels in still camera mode, the sharper your photos will turn out. For standard-size photos, 4MP (mega-pixels) will generate excellent standard-size stills.

5. High Definition (HD): In order to record and watch videos in high definition, and take full advantage of the display capabilities of your HDTV, you will need an HD camcorder. HD camcorders produce stunning clarity and are typically capable of recording in 16:9 widescreen formats.

As you will find, there are many good quality and affordable video cameras on the market to choose from and that start at just over $100. A camera's cost is dependent upon its picture quality capability, its hard drive storage capacity and other specialized features. Keep in mind that technology changes about every six months, but I recommend purchasing either a SD (standard video) or HD (high definition) camera that allows you to record directly to the camera's hard drive, has at least 20 gigabytes (gigs) of built-in 'hard-drive' storage capacity and has 'plug-and-play capability. The term 'plug-and-play' refers to your computer's ability to automatically discover any hardware component that is plugged into the computer without the need for physical device configuration. This is the easiest way to transfer the recorded material from your cameras hard drive to your computer (or storage device), since all you have to do is plug the video camera directly into your computer's USB 2.0 interface port. Once plugged in, your computer will automatically recognize the camera and easily guide you through the transfer process from your cameras video files to your computer or to the data storage device that you designate. For video cameras that record directly to a flash memory card (SD card) or directly to a DVD, your computer must have a compatible flash card port built into the computer or a DVD drive to transfer the DVD disc files to the computer.

Once your video content has been transferred to your computer, you then need to purchase a computer video editing program (software) that is compatible with your computer's operating system and know how to effectively utilize the editing program. Which software is the right one for you depends upon how much you are willing to spend, your computer's operating system and your technical ability. There are several software companies that produce video editing software, but the most recognizable names include Adobe, Corel, Apple, Pinnacle and Nero. Video-editing programs can range in price from $30 to well over $200. However, prior to purchasing the software research the internet to see if there is a 'free trial' available that you can download on-line in order to practice and make sure that you feel comfortable utilizing the program. Also, make sure that the editing program includes special effects that allow you to accentuate his ability such as spot shadows, arrows and text features; as well as, a feature that allows you the option of 'burning' a DVD copy once you are finished. Some video editing programs go further and have the capability to automatically upload the completed video onto YouTube and even onto your cellular phone.

If you do not have the time or the technical knowhow to do-it-yourself as outlined above, my advice is simple, do not cut corners nor spare any expense to help your son produce a quality highlight film. A quality highlight film could costs around $200 to $500, depending upon the time required to produce the film and the film's duration. To update an existing highlight film, it could cost between $100 to $200. Prior to spending your money, ask the professional which video editing program they utilize and if the highlight film will include arrows, spot shadows and text that will highlight your son's best plays. Also, make sure the professional you hire knows how to appropriately sequence the film and knows the difference between a 'highlight' play and an ordinary play clip not worthy of being included in the film.

> **HIGHLIGHT FILM TIP:** Have your son's highlight film professionally produced by an experienced source that is familiar with the football recruiting process, that has experience creating football highlight films and is capable of evaluating the contents of the film.

What to Do Prior to Sending Out the Highlight Film

As noted earlier, the primary goals of the highlight film is to accentuate your son's abilities, catch a coach's attention, make them want to evaluate your son further, and ultimately establish a recruiting connection. *Prior to sending out your son's highlight film for evaluation*, ensure that you always have several copies of the film on-hand and that the film is:

- Truly a polished product worthy of a college coach's evaluation.
- Evaluated for feedback by his coach(s) or a recruiting professional.
- > Sent to schools that realistically match his ability level, and always sent directly to a specific coach and immediately upon request!

- Placed on as many on-line social media outlets such as YouTube, MySpace and Facebook; as well as, recruiting Web sites like Rivals.com, Scout.com, MaxPreps, or ESPN.

Chapter 6
Contacting Coaches
And
Marketing Your Son

"One opportunity and a plan can make any dream a reality."

Dr. Todd Meiklejohn

You have heard me mention the saying that "recruiting is all about relationships." You cannot market your son and he cannot build and sustain a recruiting relationship with a college recruiter without some form of communication. All year round, college football programs expend a lot of time and effort to send out written communication, contact prospects, and promote their football programs through events such as Junior Days, Spring Games, and/or summer camps. These on-campus events are intended to not only showcase their football program, but also reach out to athletes who may be on their recruiting radar. In the recruiting process, it is important for coaches to spend as much time interacting with recruits on their campus in order to observe and evaluate how they and their family interact with the coaching staff, to further strengthen or develop relationships, and to evaluate whether the recruit is a good "fit" for the team, especially prior to extending them an offer.

Beginning in your son's ninth grade year and throughout his recruiting process, you should utilize a similar, year-round approach to proactively communicate with colleges, market your son's abilities, and showcase his talents—either through the internet, at a combine, a summer camp, or on a college campus. If you do not take these steps, others will and your son will miss vital opportunities for exposure.

> **RECRUITING TIP:** Although you and your son will reach out and contact numerous schools during his recruiting process, you only need to develop **one** successful recruiting relationship and get **one** school to fall in love with him in order to offer him a scholarship.

The relationship a recruit has with his targeted recruiter and vice-versa is the difference maker or deal breaker in whether a prospect decides to commit or sign with a particular school. Often, when a recruit is asked why he chose a particular school, the answers you hear most often are that he felt comfortable with the school's coaching staff, his recruiter was like a mentor or a "father figure" to him or that they developed a strong bond with one another during the recruiting process. These are all positive signs that the recruiter established a solid recruiting relationship between him and his targeted recruit. Again, this close bond may be the determining factor as to whether the athlete verbally commits or signs a scholarship. Developing recruiting relationships is so important to college coach's that they focus on building them year-round, spend weeks at a time away from their families, and travel thousands of miles from coast-to-coast—all in an attempt to build, strengthen, and maintain relationships with targeted recruits. As noted earlier, a coach's job security and career advancement rest heavily upon achieving two critical objectives: winning games and being a successful recruiter.

NCAA Contact Periods

With the constant pressure to win and recruit the best players year after year, one of the most scrutinized aspects of recruiting today deals with NCAA recruiting violations pertaining to college coaches contacting recruits. In fact, when cell phone texting first emerged, it became such a problem in the recruiting process that the NCAA banned all coaches from the practice altogether by the end of 2007. Today, there are strict parameters that govern the types of contact permissible by college coaches. In a perfect world, your son's high school coach would contact colleges and/or universities on his behalf in order to market him, and help him develop and maintain recruiting relationships. However, if his coach is not involved in this process, then you are charged with the responsibility of contacting schools and marketing your son.

In this section, we will focus on the various NCAA contact periods, including when the NCAA permits a college football coach to contact your son, when you are allowed to contact them, and how these different contact periods can affect your son's recruiting process. The abbreviated 'contact' recruiting calendar in Appendix E provides you with an overview of the permissible types of recruiting contact a football recruiter may have with a football prospect, specifies contact timelines and dates; as well as, the allowable number and types of contact and evaluations a coach can make based upon a recruits academic year (The NCAA, "NCAA Recruiting Chart", 2010). However, this chart is only an abbreviated version of the NCAA's recruiting calendar, so I recommend that you refer to the NCAA's Web site in order to obtain the complete version of the full "football recruiting calendar" and to determine which contact period is currently applicable to your son's stage of recruitment. You can find the NCAA's current Division I and Division II football recruiting calendars on their home Web page (www.NCAA.org) by clicking the tab:

Key Issues→Recruiting→Recruiting Calendars→Football

The NCAA forbids college coaches to engage in written correspondence (except questionnaires and camp brochures) with freshman or sophomore recruits, to call them, or to have any type of off-campus contact with them or their family. However, despite these contact restrictions, *you or your son may initiate written or phone contact with colleges (or coaches); as well as, visit their schools unofficially beginning in his ninth grade year and at any time thereafter during his high school career.*

RECRUITNG TIP: You should begin to identify, reach out to and contact colleges during your son's ninth grade year (see the RPP in Appendix F).

According to the NCAA, a *contact* occurs any time a college coach has any face-to-face contact with you or your son off a college campus, even if it is only to say "hello." A contact also occurs if a coach has any contact with your son at his high school or any location where he is competing or practicing. The four NCAA contact periods are outlined in Table 7:

Table 7 *The Four NCAA Contact Periods*

Types of Recruiting Contact	Contact Periods			
	Dead Period	Evaluation Period	Quiet Period	Contact Period
A college coach is allowed to have in-person contact with the parent or athlete **ON** the college's campus	NO	NO	NO	YES
A college coach is allowed to have in-person contact with the parent or athlete **OFF** of the college's campus	NO	NO	NO	YES
A college coach is allowed to write the parent or athlete	YES	YES	YES	YES
A college coach is allowed to call the parent or athlete	YES	YES	YES	YES
A college coach is allowed to watch the athlete play and visit their school	NO	YES	NO	YES
The parent and athlete may make 'un-official' visits to college campuses	YES	YES	YES	YES
Cell phone texting allowed	NO	NO	NO	NO

The exact number (Example: the number of telephone calls) and types of contact permitted by a college coach with a recruit differs by an athlete's grade, by sport and by the contact period. The contact period dates change from year-to-year. Refer to the NCAA's Web site in order to obtain the complete version of the "football recruiting calendar" and to determine which current contact period is applicable to your son's grade level and stage of recruitment.

Receiving College Correspondence

September 1st of your son's junior year is the official date he can begin receiving college correspondence such as recruiting materials (i.e. letters, questionnaires, invitations to visit) from NCAA Division I and Division II football programs. Receiving college correspondence is a crucial element in his recruiting process and a good sign because once he starts receiving correspondence, he can begin developing and strengthening relationships with schools or college recruiters, which will help your son become more focused with his recruiting efforts.

RECRUITING TIP: Any time your son reaches out to a school or college coach, by returning a questionnaire, by phone or written correspondence or by sending them a copy of his highlight film for evaluation, it may lead to a recruiting connection or relationship between him and the school.

If your son receives a recruiting (prospect) questionnaire from a school, *always make sure you or he completely fills out the questionnaire and sends it back to the school (postage is generally free) within twenty-four hours*. On the other hand, if your son is interested in a particular school, I recommend that he not wait for a letter in the mail and that he visit the team's Web site to fill out their recruiting questionnaire online. By proactively going online to fill out questionnaires and returning them expeditiously through the mail, it will ensure that the school receives his current academic, personal, and athletic information for their recruiting database. This can lead to future correspondence or a decision to evaluate him more in-depth.

How to Create an Athletic (Player) Profile

Prior to sending a coach your son's highlight film or contacting them, it is imperative to develop his *"player profile."* A player profile is essentially your son's athletic resume and, therefore, another vital recruiting tool his recruiting plan. Like a job resume, the player profile makes a first impression; introduces an athlete to a coach, describes their background and details their accomplishments both on and off of the field. More importantly, this key recruiting tool (along with the highlight film) can help an athlete establish a recruiting relationship and gain exposure. So, ensure that your son creates a quality player profile, one that is a polished product and free of any content or grammatical errors, since you only get one chance to make a good first impression! In Appendix J, you will find a sample player profile to assist your son with the development of his own. An athlete's player profile should include their:

- *Contact Information:* Their current address, home and cell phone number, and email address.

- *Parent(s) Contact Information:* Their home number(s) and cell phone number(s) and email addresses.

- *Head Coaches Contact Information:* Their school phone number, cell number, and email address.

- *Academic Information:* Include the athlete's current GPA, ACT or SAT scores, any honors, gifted, or AP courses they have taken or plan to take, academic awards; as well as, their ten digit NCAA Clearinghouse registration number.

- *Athletic Accomplishments*: List any individual or cumulative playing statistics by year (be honest), honors and awards, records broken, team accomplishments (state/district championships), and other sports played.

- *Picture*: Include a quality high-resolution photo from the shoulders up, also called a head shot.

Finally, create his profile utilizing a common computer program such as Microsoft Word and check the document for grammatical errors and proper sentence structure prior to sending out the document. If your son's profile contains grammatical errors, is not legible, or sent via email utilizing an obscure word processing program, it will make a bad first impression and frustrate a coach if they are unable to open and/or read the document. This could cause the coach to disregard the email and your efforts would have been wasted.

It is also important that your son have his vital recruiting tools on-hand when the opportunity presents itself in order to effectively market his abilities. This means always attaching an up-to-date copy of his player profile to any highlight film or to any written correspondences between you (or your son) and a college recruiter, when passing his film out to members of the recruiting media or when attending football events. During an athlete's senior year, I also recommend that they keep in their book bag; at least five packets containing copies of their highlight film, player profile, unofficial transcript and a copy of their latest SAT or ACT score, in the event that they receive a visit from a college recruiter at school. Again, the opportunity for exposure, to make a good first impression and/or establish a recruiting connection does not come around often for recruits so it is important for them to be prepared and make the most of each moment.

How to Gather College Contact Information

If your son is not receiving serious recruiting interest or correspondence of any sort by September 1 of his junior year, then you need to take an aggressive approach when it comes to promoting him to schools. This means contacting coaches via phone, written correspondence, and by email.

With the advent of technology, email is obviously much faster and may prove to be more beneficial when sending large amounts of specific information, such as your son's player profile, updated news bits, and online links to his highlight film. However, you must first know how to gather the contact information for the targeted schools. To begin, simply input the school's name followed by the word "football" in a random Google search. This should produce the school's official athletic Web page. Once you are on the school's athletic site, locate their 'football' home page and find the list of coaches on staff under either the tab titled 'coaching staff' or 'roster'. Once you locate the coach's directory, find the teams *"recruiting coordinator"*. The recruiting coordinator is either an assistant coach or a football staff member who is responsible for organizing the coaches recruiting efforts and overseeing all recruiting functions including player visits, identifying and evaluating potential prospects, and coordinating recruiting correspondence. However, smaller division schools may not have a recruiting coordinator. If this is the case, identify your son's position coach or the coach that recruits the geographical area in which you reside. Each coach's bio page should list their email and phone contact information.

The school's football mailing address is generally found on the football departments home Web page or in the school's "athletic/staff directory". In the athletic/staff directory, you will again find a list of all of the football coaches, their contact information, and other football personnel, including the head coach's administrative secretary (if they have one). Once you have obtained the necessary contact information, I recommend that you call the school's football office directly in order to verify the contact information or to obtain any information you did not find on their Web site. This is necessary since you will want to ensure that the school receives your son's highlight film or any other written correspondence. If your son has received recent football correspondence from schools, you can find the school contact information directly on the school's letterhead and on the envelope.

RECRUITING TIP: Never throw away any recruiting letters that your son receives until you have recorded the school's and coach's contact information for your records.

This book includes a contact log in Appendix M to help you record pertinent college contact information, build your database of college contacts and help you get organized with your contacts.

Essential Recruiting Supplies

In your quest to establish even one recruiting relationship, you may be required to target and contact hundreds of schools. Being organized and having the right recruiting supplies to assist you with your efforts is crucial to your success. Prior to contacting schools, there are some expenses you must be prepared to pay for and essential supplies you will need to purchase. This includes, but is not limited to:

1. Blank reams of DVDs to burn copies of your son's highlight film.
2. DVD labels and blank copy paper.
3. Shipping supplies including stamps, 6 x 9 envelopes, and shipping labels.
4. Fed Ex or overnight shipping expenses.
5. Extra fuel money for repeated trips to the local post office.

Suggestions on How and When to Market Your Son

Now that you know how to obtain a college's contact information and you have your supplies (including his highlight film and player profile), it is time to reach out to college football programs and market your son (and his abilities) to gain their attention. Keep in mind that this task will be time consuming, may be expensive, and at times frustrating but well worth the effort. As noted earlier, in order to effectively market your son's abilities, you must be prepared to spend time targeting and obtaining contact information on hundreds of compatible or interested schools, and regularly send them the latest copy of your son's highlight film and email updates on his progress or accomplishments. This year-round process begins in your son's ninth grade year and does not officially end until he signs his National Letter of Intent (NLI). However, this process may eventually slow down once he starts receiving offers and/or makes a verbal commitment.

In your son's quest for exposure, his marketing is not just limited to contacting colleges and universities. You will also want to focus your attention on contacting and sending his information to the national recruiting media such as Rivals.com, MaxPreps, Scout.com, and other regional or local recruiting media in your area. You can easily find representatives from the recruiting media on-line, at your local combine, at football camps or any number of other football related functions. In my area of South Florida, thousands of parents and prospects each year turn to Larry Bluestein of the *Miami Herald* for his assistance and his insight. Larry is a trusted and important high school football recruiting resource in the area and has covered the sport for almost forty years. He is well respected, sincere, and is always willing to help.

Another marketing option to consider is turning to other area high school coaches for assistance and asking them if they can recommend your son to their college contacts. When making their recruiting rounds, it is not uncommon for a college recruiter to inquire about other area prospects that a coach may know about, but is not from his school. Other area high school coaches may be familiar with your son's talents and may be willing to assist him or help promote him to their college contacts.

Utilizing Technology to Promote Your Son

In your quest to contact schools, utilize all available technological options at your disposal.

> **RECRUITING TIP:** Technology significantly expedites the contact process. If you do not have access to the latest technology or are limited in your technological abilities, find someone competent to assist you and/or go out and purchase the latest communication tools for the task at hand.

These days an investment in the latest mobile device, computer equipment or video technology may pay big dividends toward helping your son develop a quality highlight film, connect him to a school or help him get noticed. At a minimum, have a dependable computer with decent hard drive storage and updated software, separate email addresses for you and your son, high speed Internet access, and a mobile device that can multi-task. Essentially, today's "smart phone" (mobile phone), I Pad, or Internet tablet can function as a portable mini-computer, capable of advanced computing abilities such as:

1. Uploading/downloading images or documents directly from the device
2. Sending and receiving emails
3. Surfing the Web at high speeds
4. Connecting you to numerous online social mediums that college football programs now utilize such as Facebook, Twitter, My Space and YouTube to name a few.

In your son's quest to get his information out quickly and gain exposure, you will want to employ all technological means necessary during his recruiting process.

Contacting Coaches by Written Correspondence (or Email)

Truth is college coaches are glad to hear from a prospect at anytime, especially if the prospect is talented and can help their program win. Like a prospect's highlight film, the intended outcome of reaching out and contacting a coach is to get their attention and generate interest so that the coach will want to learn more about your son and return contact with him. However, prior to contacting a college coach, first consider the time of the year. For example, football is a fall sport and coaches are extremely busy during the actual football season. On the other hand, making contact in the early spring, say during early March may prove to be more beneficial. Also, make sure that the schools you or your son are attempting to contact realistically match his ability level and they are schools that have actually shown an interest in him.

When contacting a school by written correspondence, always send them a copy of your son's current highlight (or game) film and his player profile. Today, emailing coaches is obviously the quickest and easiest way to send a written correspondence, send an update or stay in touch with them. However, sending an email to a coach may prove ineffective if the coach does not regularly check or respond to his email and if his email is not directly linked to his cell phone. Most recruiters today cannot afford not to have a mobile phone that is capable of receiving email directly to their phone, but those that do, can get an overwhelming number of emails, regardless of the time of year. Sometimes your son's written correspondence can get lost in the mix and directed to another support staff member other than the intended coach; a coach may be busy, may not be permitted by NCAA rules to return the contact, or he simply may not choose to respond. Regardless, do not get discouraged and do not stop trying.

The contents of any written correspondence should be specific, concise, unique, and remain on-going during the recruiting process. Contacting and updating coaches once a month via email is common during the recruiting process, but *never inundate a coach with too many letters, emails or phone calls*. When sending written correspondence to a college coach, athletes should include:

- The name of the coach, and the college or university they represent
- Their player profile
- The name of their high school, its address and phone number
- The name of their head coach and position coach; as well as, the coach's contact information
- Their current athletic information, accomplishments, any recent game/team updates or re-caps, achievements, and any awards or honors they recently received
- Their current academic information including their core GPA or a qualifying score on the ACT or SAT exam and year of graduation
- Any online links that posted their highlight film such as YouTube and/or recruiting Web sites

Always conclude the correspondence with a "thank you" to the coach and an invitation to your son's campus. Finally, check the spelling, grammar, and punctuation of the correspondence prior to sending the correspondence.

Contacting Coaches by Phone

Contacting a coach by phone is the most direct form of communication, but it is also not an exact science. As noted earlier, there are NCAA rules that regulate a coach's phone contact with your son. Although a coach may not contact your son by phone in either his ninth or tenth grade year, you both may initiate any form of contact with a coach at anytime and as frequently as you or he would like once your son enters the ninth grade.

Making phone contact with a coach is vital, so in order to make a good first impression and the most of this opportunity, your son must be prepared, confident and concise. I recommend that your son develop a list of relevant questions to ask the coach, rehearse each question; as well as, rehearse the answers he will give. In addition, it is important to make sure that your son writes down the answers to each question and any pertinent information that the coach relays to him so that later, he can recall the important details of their conversation. During a phone conversation with a college coach, short or unintelligible responses and/or pauses will not win the favor of a coach. To help your son develop relevant questions to ask a college coach, he may want to formulate his questions based upon the following criteria:

- Does the school actively recruit in his geographical area and do they currently have players on their roster from his high school and/or the area?
- What is the stability of the coaching staff?—how long has the head coach; as well as, the other coaches been on staff at the school?
- Any questions pertaining to academics, such as player graduation rates, admission requirements, the school's various degree programs, the school's enrollment, average class sizes, professor-to-student ratios, athlete academic support services and academic assistance.
- The typical player schedule during the season, including his academic schedule and his schedule in the off-season including the summer break.
- Questions related to the school's campus, including the type of town it is located in, the team's training facilities, the player's housing facilities, and student life on campus.
- How many players are currently on their roster at his position and is there an opportunity to play immediately?

- Can you and your son arrange an 'unofficial visit' and take a tour if permitted? (always ask)

- Can the coach send your son general information about the school and the football program?

Now that these preliminaries have been established, ensure that your son:

1. Targets school's that realistically match his ability level both athletically and academically.

2. Contacts school's first (prioritize) that have shown an interest in him, have sent him written correspondence, or that actively recruit either at his school or in your area.

3. Role-play the intended phone conversation with you, a teammate or a friend.

Again, as your son's recruiting efforts progress, it is important to be organized and maintain a database of every college (and the coach's name) that has contacted your son, or that you have made contact with, along with the dates, the contact information and various notes containing relevant information gained from conversations with coaches. In Appendix M, you will find a contact log to help you establish a recruiting database and record pertinent contact information.

Visiting Schools

At some point during your son's recruiting process, you and he will take *unofficial* visits to a variety of schools and he may be invited to take an *official* visit. Visiting schools is another vital form of contact; as well as, a critical component in his marketing process that could lead to him receiving a scholarship offer. Not to mention, it is a key marketing tool utilized by colleges to showcase their football program and an opportunity for the coaches to again build relationships with targeted recruits or secure commitments. For you and your son, it is a great opportunity to experience the college atmosphere, view the team's facilities, find out what the school has to offer, spend time building (or enhancing) your relationship with the coaches, and it should help your son begin to narrow his choice of schools. However, prior to any campus visit, ensure that you and son are prepared for the visit by doing some background research on both the school and its football (athletic) program.

As supported in the RPP in Appendix F, the un-official visitation process should begin during your son's freshman year. In addition, you and your son may make as many unofficial visits to a school as you would like. An *unofficial visit* is considered any visit by a prospect to a college campus paid for by themselves or their family. The only expense you may receive on behalf of a college or a university is three complimentary tickets to a regular season home game. If your son receives an invitation to a schools' regular season game, a spring game, or a 'Junior Day' the invitation generally includes specific instructions for him to RSVP ahead of time so that he can be placed on an official list to secure his seats. Again, unofficial visits are a perfect opportunity to promote your son by hand delivering his player profile and highlight film directly to the coaching staff; as well as, start building a relationship with a school that has expressed an interest in him, extended him an offer, or that is seriously recruiting him. Never miss the opportunity to take an unofficial visit should a school in fact extend your son this privileged opportunity. On the other hand, be wary of traveling far or spending a lot of money on an un-official visit if a school has not extended him an invitation or has shown your son little, if any, recruiting interest.

Once your son begins his senior year, he may take five official visits to separate schools, providing a school officially extends him an invitation to visit. An official visit may last up to two days and the college or university may pay for the following expenses:

- A recruits transportation to and from the college (generally airfare)
- His room and meals (three per day) while visiting
- Reasonable entertainment expenses, including three complimentary tickets to a home game

IMPORTANT NCAA REQUIREMENT: Before your son takes an official visit to an NCAA Division I institution, he must provide the school with a copy of his high school transcript, SAT/ACT score and he must be registered with the NCAA Eligibility Center (The NCAA Clearinghouse).

Chapter 7
Combines and Football Camps

"Some people dream of success, while others wake up and work hard at it."

Fred Shero
Two-time NHL Stanley
Cup Winning Coach

About Combines

With big corporate entities behind these events such as NIKE and Under Armor, combines and related football events have gained popularity in the world of high school football recruiting in recent years and are now a fixture in the off-season. The promoters of certain combines can now advertise that several current NFL players and top draft picks attended their combine while they were in high school. However, the pros and cons of these events are a topic of great debate. Proponents would argue that a combine is a popular way to market your son and help him gain exposure if he in fact has a stellar performance and catches the eye of the recruiting media. Detractors would argue that exposure at these events is not a certainty since some events do little or nothing to actually promote your son's true football abilities to college coaches. In fact, the NCAA prohibits college coaches from attending these events in order to scout prospects. Furthermore, others might argue that college coaches place little credence on how well a prospect actually performs at a combine in comparison to their summative evaluation of that prospect. In other words, if a prospect is truly that gifted and a established player, then he really does not have to prove himself any further at an off season event to gain exposure or to receive a scholarship.

Regardless of the debate, I recommend that your son attend at least two combines each year from the spring of his freshman year to the spring of his junior year in order to gauge his physical development, improve his skill sets, compete against other local talent and of course as an opportunity for exposure. The combine season typically runs from January through July and each event lasts about three hours (from the early morning until the early afternoon). The combine regimen consist of mostly timed skill events that include a 40-yard dash, an agility shuttle, a measured broad or vertical jump, and concludes with some type of one-on-one skills competitions.

Combines *worth* attending:

- Are FREE such as:
  - **NIKE**: http://www.nike.com/nikeos/p/sparqtraining/en_US/
  - **Under Armor**: http://combines.underarmour.com
- Help expose prospects to local or national recruiting media.
- Allow parents and athletes the opportunity to network with the recruiting media and submit copies of their highlight films and player information.
- Provide prospects with useful recruiting information and/or parents with some type of academic/recruiting seminar that will assist their son's recruiting efforts (not a short sales pitch from a recruiting service).
- Provide an opportunity for prospects to attend a related showcase event for free.
- Allow prospects the opportunity to compete with the area's best competition.

Be wary of football events that do not deliver and:

- Are EXPENSIVE. The going rate to participate in a combine is typically FREE, but a worthwhile event could cost between $30 - $60, providing the event offers many of the benefits outlined above. Football camps may range from $100 to $400.
- Do not assist prospects with their recruiting efforts or exposure.
- Attempt to sell you expensive recruiting services, unnecessary merchandise, training equipment, or nutritional supplements.

On another note, **NEVER** allow your son to take part in an all-star game that charges you money in order for him to participate. All-star games are a great opportunity for senior's prospects to gain exposure and showcase their talents one last time, especially for those individuals who have no scholarship offers. Typically, players are invited based upon their athletic accomplishments. In turn, the individual(s) sponsoring the event should pay all costs associated with hosting the event.

About Showcase Events

At some combines such as NIKE, prospects will have the opportunity to earn an invitation to a more exclusive football event known as a *showcase* event. A showcase event is another type of physical evaluation or football skills camp reserved only for the top-rated high school prospects. This event is typically by invitation only, and hosted by a college, a nationally recognized recruiting organization, or a company affiliated with high school football. If your son is fortunate enough to receive an invitation to a prominent showcase event, never turn down the opportunity to attend. Particularly, since the local and national recruiting media heavily cover these events and it is a great platform for your son to further showcase and promote his abilities. Not to mention, these opportunities do not come around often. Ultimately, if your son is going to prove that he ranks among the best of the best at his position, he should never shy away from competing on any stage at the highest level, whether it is on game day, at a combine, or at a football camp. More importantly, he should train appropriately prior to any skills competition and show up in the best condition possible, both mentally and physically.

How to Choose a Summer Camp

Like combines, summer football camps are another important part of an athlete's recruiting process particularly during their freshman and sophomore years when they are looking to develop their skill sets, network with college coaches, visit an actual college campus or simply attract the attention of a college coach. For college coaches, summer camps are another opportunity to identify new recruiting prospects and evaluate prospects that are currently on their radar.

As outlined in the RPP in Appendix F, I recommend that athletes attend summer football camps as early as their freshman year since they may prove to be a rewarding experience and a legitimate platform for them to gain exposure and further develop at their position. However, attending summer camps can cost parents hundreds, if not thousands of dollars when you add up the camp's cost and travel expenses, and which camp(s) to attend depends upon several factors since athletes may receive hundreds of college camp invitations throughout their recruiting process. In order to decide which camp is right for your son and ensure that his camp experience is worthwhile, consider the following:

- The camp's cost
- You and your son's summer schedule
- Location and related travel expenses
- The quality of the camp staff (are they a high school or a college coach staff?)
- Will the camp benefit your son's skill development
- Is the school hosting the camp seriously recruiting your son?
- If the school is not seriously recruiting your son, should he attend anyway because it is his dream school and he wants to go for it?
- Would a one-day camp be more beneficial?

Ultimately, consider the developmental aspects of the camp based on your son's current ability level. In other words, how much will he benefit from attending the camp and will the benefits outweigh the costs?

Chapter 8
Off-the-Field Behavior, Character, and Parent Behavior

"For an athlete…nothing good ever happens after midnight."

Unknown Author

Today, there are thousands of prospects competing for only a limited number of scholarship opportunities. College coaches work tirelessly in order to evaluate every aspect of a prospects potential; as well as, assess which prospects are worthy of scholarship considerations, their sacrifice, their time and of course, a scholarship offer. With so much at stake, you can expect college coaches to scrutinize every aspect of your son's life including his character, his academic and school disciplinary history and your family's background. Needless to say, your son can severely damage his chances of earning an athletic scholarship or an offer altogether by getting into trouble at school, with the law and/or by abusing drugs (including steroids) and alcohol.

Athletic Ability vs. Character

There is a consensus among recruiters that if your son does not exercise sound discipline and good decision-making during high school both on and off the field, then he will most likely run the risk of exhibiting the same detrimental behaviors during college.

What may have taken years to build can dissolve within minutes as news of your son's negative behavior or arrest spreads quickly over the Internet and on other forms of online social media such as Twitter and Facebook. The school's head football coach is typically the highest paid employee on campus, a highly visible public figure and will not jeopardize his job or the future of his football program because of negative publicity associated with a recruit's controversial behavior or legal troubles, regardless as to how good he as a player.

WARNING: Although everybody makes mistakes when they are young, breaking the law or not adhering to the established rules during the recruiting process CAN COST YOUR SON EVERYTHING (even if it is only one time).

In the recruiting process, ability does not trump character and talent will only take your son so far. Today, coaches scout athletes not only to evaluate their athletic and academic abilities, but also to assess intangibles such as their on-field and sideline behavior, dedication level, work ethic and even how they treat their parents. Specific attributes they look for when scouting an athlete might include cursing, yelling at teammates, complaining, and effort levels during both practice and in games. *In a recruiters final evaluation and when it is time for the head coach to decide whether they will or will not extend a scholarship offer, your son's ability will not outweigh his "character" attributes (or lack thereof).*

Parent Behavior

Parents are not exempt from a college recruiter's scrutiny during the recruiting process. Simply put, your character, attitude, and actions can negatively affect your son's chances for a scholarship or an offer. Not to rip on little league soccer or the many fine and decent parents who attend soccer games to support their children's efforts, but the term "soccer parent," unfortunately, is now a cliché term for any annoying or disruptive parent on the sidelines. As a parent and a role model, you can help your sons recruiting efforts if you:

1. Cheer and not coach. Avoid yelling specific instructions or issuing commands during a contest.

2. Avoid running up and down the sidelines shouting. Don't distract the players or block the view of other spectators.

3. Keep negative comments to yourself.

4. Do not yell at, curse, or argue with the referee's, linesmen, or the opposition.

5. Stand, or sit, at least three to five yards back from the sidelines.

6. *Respect* your son's coaches as well as college recruiters. This means not questioning the coaches play calling or personnel decisions, issuing unnecessary demands, ultimatums, or scrutinizing a college recruiter as to why they may not be pursuing your son and/or offering him a scholarship.

Unfortunately, most of us have witnessed a parent in the stands, constantly yelling, flaring up at the referees, opposing players, and even at their own kid. They are flat out annoying, as they repeatedly question the coach's play calling or his aptitude for the game and/or the referee's penalty calls. Parental rage has been studied closely in recent years. However, there is little data to explain why parents erupt in anger (or violence) at a sporting event, despite the fact that is happening more often. Regardless, always conduct yourself accordingly since you are the adult and you never know when and where a college recruiter may be present and/or observing your behavior. More importantly, always remember that 'it is just a game'!

Epilogue

If you think you are beaten you are; if you think you dare not, you don't; if you want to win but think you can't; it's almost a cinch you won't.

If you think you'll lose you're lost; for out of the world we find success begins with a fellow's will; it's all in a state of mind.

Life's battles don't always go to the stronger and faster man, but sooner or later the man who wins is the man who thinks he can.

Unknown Author

My high school coach once read us this inspirational quote after practice one day before a big playoff game as we made our way to the state finals my junior year. The quote and its meaning are open to interpretation, but what I learned more than anything from his speech that day was—you have to believe in yourself first and foremost, but in our case, we had to envision winning the game way before we ever touched the field. Steven Covey summed it up perfectly by stating, "begin with the end in mind." Your son's success in his recruiting process is no different. You will find, as I did, that if you or your son believe at any moment that he cannot obtain a scholarship, then he will not.

If you take anything away from this book, I hope that you remember to have a recruiting plan for your son and to start his recruiting process early (do not procrastinate). More importantly, becoming a serious minded student-athlete dedicated to obtaining an athletic scholarship starts as early as middle school. In other words, his recruiting process is a marathon and not a sprint, it is as much about its journey as it is its destination and it is a road filled with many peaks and valleys. I also warned you earlier that the recruiting process is not an exact science and the rules constantly change. Never think for a moment that there is a short cut or a 'silver bullet' (easy way) toward obtaining a scholarship. Obtaining an athletic scholarship today requires a tremendous amount of sacrifice on your son's behalf and will require you to go above and beyond to help him achieve this once in a lifetime opportunity.

Remember not to put all of your eggs in one basket and although this book will serve as a valuable recruiting resource to you and your son, keep in mind that no book, person, or recruiting service can guarantee that your son will receive a football scholarship. More importantly, *YOU, not your son's coach, are his greatest recruiting asset* since more than likely; you will find yourself taking a hands-on, do-it-yourself approach toward helping him make it to the next level. I wrote this book with the belief that if your son starts his recruiting process early, has good grades and ability, has a recruiting plan, and you employ the strategies outlined throughout this guide, he will have a happy conclusion to his recruiting process.

Although this guide speaks to you as the parent responsible for your son's recruiting process, it is important to note that when it comes to the actual work involved, you should not do everything, nor control his entire recruiting process. Ultimately, the final decision as to which college your son chooses to attend should be his decision. However, you (or other family members) and your son must work as a team and make time to perform recruiting tasks together. As a parent who has personally gone through this lengthy journey, there will be many times when you will need your son's feedback and his opinions regarding his wants, his needs, and his direction. It is your job to make your son feel that his input and/or ideas are valued. You and he will learn together and share together in this recruiting experience. In the end, a team approach will draw you closer as a family, you will get much more accomplished, be much more productive and your recruiting experience will be much more rewarding.

I intended for this book to be my legacy as an educator, but that will only happen if it first becomes a genuine educational resource for those that read it and only if it positively affects an athlete's recruiting efforts in one way or another. Regardless, I hope you enjoyed reading this book, found it easy to read, and it serves you and your son well. I hope that you refer the book to family or a friend that is in need and who is headed down their own recruiting trail. I encourage you to send me your and your son's recruiting testimonial and/or your feedback about the book. If you ever need assistance, contact us through our Web site: www.recruitingdoctor.com.

Best regards,

Dr. Todd S. Meiklejohn
'The Recruiting Doctor'

References

The NCAA. "Divsion Levels," 2010. The official Web site of the NCAA: http://www.ncaa.org (accessed April 7, 2010).

The NCAA. "Recruiting Definitions," 2010. The official Web site of the NCAA: http://www.ncaa.org (accessed March 16, 2010).

The NCAA. "NCAA Recruiting Chart," 2010. The official Web site of the NCAA: http://www.ncaa.org (accessed February 24, 2010).

Web Sites

NCAA Web Sites

The National Collegiate Athletic Association (NCAA):
http://www.ncaa.org

NCAA Eligibility Center: http://www.eligibilitycenter.org

NCAA Clearing House: http://www.ncaaclearinghouse.net

NCAA National Letter of Intent: http://www.national-letter.org

SAT/ACT Web Sites

SAT Exam: http://www.CollegeBoard.com

ACT Exam: http://www.ACT.org

SAT/ACT Preparation: http://www.kaptest.com

College Football Sites

Division 2 Football: http://www.d2football.com

Division 3 Football: http://www.d3football.com

The NAIA: http://naia.cstv.com

California's Community College Athletic Association (CCCAA):
http://www.coasports.org

The National Junior College Athletic Association (NJCAA):
http://www.njcaa.org

College Financial Aid Sites

U.S. Department of Education: http://www.fafsa.ed.gov

Federal Student Aid Information Center: http://studentaid.ed.gov

Department of Education's Direct Loan Web Site:
http://www2.ed.gov/offices/OSFAP/DirectLoan/index.html

Stafford Loan Web site: http://www.staffordloan.com

State Student Incentive Grants and Federal PLUS Loans:
http://www.parentplusloan.com

FREE Combines

NIKE: http://www.nike.com/nikeos/p/sparqtraining/en_US/

Under Armor: http://combines.underarmour.com

Glossary of Terms

ACT Exam (American College Testing Exam) – One of the two official standardized test recognized by the NCAA for eligibility purposes and college admissions.

Combine – A physical evaluation for high school football prospects designed to assess a player's speed, strength, and agility. Typically, combine events are held in the off-season from January until early July.

Core Course (Core Class) – A specific high school course that officially meets the NCAA's eligibility requirements.

Core Course Grade Point Average (Core Course GPA) – A prospective student athlete's official grade point average for eligibility purposes that is calculated based on a 4.0 scale from only NCAA approved core courses.

Correspondence – Any mail sent by colleges or universities to prospective athletes.

Grayshirt – The recruiting term used to describe a student-athlete who signs a letter of intent in February, but delays their college enrollment until the winter or spring term at their chosen institution instead of the traditional fall term.

Green Shirt – The term applied to a high school senior athlete that forgoes their spring semester in high school to enroll in college in January and participate in spring football practice.

Junior Day – A one-day event, hosted by a college football program in the springtime for selected junior prospects and their family members. A typical Junior Day includes an overview about the school, their academic programs, the coaches, and includes a tour of the team's football facilities. A Junior Day is considered an unofficial visit for a prospect.

National Signing Day – The official day permitted by the NCAA, usually in the first week of February each year, when football recruits are officially allowed to sign a National Letter of Intent (NLI) with their chosen college or university.

NCAA Clearinghouse – The official branch of the NCAA's Eligibility Center where all prospective student-athletes are required to register (junior year) if they desire to attend an affiliating institution. This branch of the NCAA is responsible for maintaining all athletes' official academic information as it pertains to eligibility requirements.

Offer (Written Offer, Scholarship Offer) – An unofficial scholarship offer extended to a prospect on behalf of a college or university prior to national signing day. Neither a prospect nor a school is obligated to an offer.

Official Transcript – The official high school document that lists all of the high school courses taken by a student-athlete, including the grades received for each course and their current weighted and un-weighted grade point averages. In addition, this official document *must* be forwarded to both the NCAA's Clearinghouse and any selected university's admission office upon request.

On-the-Radar – A common recruiting term that refers to a prospect who is experiencing positive recruiting signs, who may be well known by the recruiting media or college coaches, and is typically being seriously considered for a scholarship.

Player Profile (Athletic Resume) – A comprehensive document (and recruiting tool) created by a player that details and provides an overview of their current academic, athletic, and personal information (see Appendix J).

Prospect or Recruit – The most common recruiting terms utilized by college coaches and the recruiting media that refers to a high school student-athlete.

PSAT – The Preliminary SAT/National Merit Scholarship Qualifying Test (PSAT/NMSQT) is a standardized test taken by sophomores prior to the SAT. The test is administered by the College Board and National Merit Scholarship Corporation (NMSC) and consist of three sections: Math, Critical Reading, and Writing Skills.

Qualifier (NCAA Qualifier) – A high school student-athlete officially eligible by all NCAA standards, qualified to receive an NCAA scholarship and play at the NCAA level.

Questionnaire (Recruiting Questionnaire) – A recruiting form used by college football programs to collect important (current) prospect information pertaining to their academics, athletics, and personal information. A recruiting questionnaire is either mailed to a prospect through correspondence or found online at the school's athletic Web site.

Recruiter (College Recruiter) – The term that refers to a college coach who recruits prospective high school athletes.

Recruiting Professional – A term used in this guide that refers to any individual who represents a recruiting service and who provides high school football recruiting product or services.

Redshirt – When an athlete is granted one extra year of NCAA eligibility due to an injury or insufficient playing time. Being designated a redshirt allows an athlete a total of five years to obtain their bachelor's degree. Upon being designated as a redshirt, an athlete is allowed to attend classes and practice, but cannot participate in athletic contents during their redshirt season.

SAT Exam (The SAT Reasoning Test) - One of the two official standardized test recognized by the NCAA for eligibility purposes and college admissions (formerly known as the Scholastic Aptitude Test and Scholastic Assessment Test).

Showcase Event – An off-season football skills camp, typically reserved for only top-rated high school prospect's, hosted by a college or university, a nationally recognized recruiting organization or a company associated with high school football recruiting. A showcase event is typically 'invitation only'.

Sliding Scale – The NCAA's official eligibility scale that matches a required core course grade point average to a specified ACT/SAT test score (see Appendices C and D).

Top-Rated Prospect (Blue Chip Prospect) – A prospect who has been identified as an elite football player by the local or national recruiting media and given a ranking as being one of the best players at his position or one of the best overall prospects available in his designated recruiting class. Typically, this prospect also holds multiple scholarship offers.

Transcript Credit Analysis – A formal and comprehensive analysis of a high school transcript conducted by a qualified guidance counselor to determine a student's grade point average, if the student-athlete is taking and meeting the required NCAA core class requisites, and is on schedule to graduate in eight academic semesters.

Under-Exposed (Off-the-Radar) – Refers to a prospect who is unknown by the recruiting media or by college coaches and is generally not being seriously considered for a scholarship. This prospect also typically has no scholarship offers.

Verbal Commitment – This recruiting term refers to a prospect's verbal promise to attend a specific college or university prior to national signing day. A verbal commitment is not binding on behalf of the prospects or the school.

529 College Savings Plan – Any college savings plan operated by a state or educational institution that helps families set aside funds for future college costs. It is named after Section 529 of the Internal Revenue Code, which created these types of savings plans in 1996.

Appendixes

Appendix A

NCAA Division I - CORE COURSE LOG COURSE and CORE GPA CALCULATOR

Grade Point Values: A=4, B=3, C=2, D=1, F=0

English (4 years)			
Course Title	Credit	X Grade =	Quality Points
Example: English 6	1	A	(1 x 4) = 4
1.			
2.			
3.			
4.			
		Total:	

Mathematics (3 years, Algebra 1 or higher)			
Course Title	Credit	X Grade =	Quality Points
Example: Algebra 1	1	B	(1 x 3) = 3
1.			
2.			
3.			
		Total:	

Natural/Physical Science (2 years, 1 must be a lab)			
Course Title	Credit	X Grade =	Quality Points
1.			
2.			
		Total:	

One (1) year additional English, Math, or Natural Physical Science			
Course Title	Credit	X Grade =	Quality Points
1.			
		Total:	

Social Science (2 years)			
Course Title	Credit	X Grade =	Quality Points
1.			
2.			
		Total:	

four (4) years of additional courses (from any above or a foreign language, non-doctrinal Religion/Philosophy, or Computer Science)			
Course Title	Credit	X Grade =	Quality Points
1.			
2.			
3.			
4.			
		Total:	

Cumulative Core GPA Calculator

Total Quality Points	(divided)	Total Credits	Cumulative GPA

Appendix B

NCAA Division II - CORE COURSE LOG COURSE and CORE GPA CALCULATOR

Grade Point Values: A=4, B=3, C=2, D=1, F=0

English (3 years)			
Course Title	**Credit**	**X Grade =**	**Quality Points**
Example: English 6	1	A	(1 x 4) = 4
1.			
2.			
3.			
		Total:	

Mathematics (2 years, Algebra 1 or higher)			
Course Title	**Credit**	**X Grade =**	**Quality Points**
Example: Algebra 1	1	B	(1 x 3) = 3
1.			
2.			
		Total:	

Natural/Physical Science (2 years, 1 must be a lab)			
Course Title	**Credit**	**X Grade =**	**Quality Points**
1.			
2.			
		Total:	

Two (2) years additional English, Math, or Natural Physical Science			
Course Title	**Credit**	**X Grade =**	**Quality Points**
1.			
2.			
		Total:	

Social Science (2 years)			
Course Title	**Credit**	**X Grade =**	**Quality Points**
1.			
2.			
3.			
		Total:	

Three (3) years of additional courses (from any above or a foreign language, non-doctrinal Religion/Philosophy, or Computer Science)			
Course Title	**Credit**	**X Grade =**	**Quality Points**
1.			
2.			
3.			
		Total:	

Cumulative Core GPA Calculator

Total Quality Points	(divided)	Total Credits	Cumulative GPA

Appendix C

NCAA DIVISION I SLIDING SCALE
(2.775 GPA - 3.550 GPA and Above)

Core GPA	SAT Verbal and Math ONLY	ACT *Score
3.550 & above	400	37
3.525	410	38
3.500	420	39
3.475	430	40
3.450	440	41
3.425	450	41
3.400	460	42
3.375	470	42
3.350	480	43
3.325	490	44
3.300	500	44
3.275	510	45
3.250	520	46
3.225	530	46
3.200	540	47
3.175	550	47
3.150	560	48
3.125	570	49
3.100	580	49
3.075	590	50
3.050	600	50
3.025	610	51
3.000	620	52
2.975	630	52
2.950	640	53
2.925	650	53
2.900	660	54
2.875	670	55
2.850	680	56
2.825	690	56
2.800	700	57
2.775	710	58

* To get an ACT 'composite score', divide the score above by (4)

Appendix D

NCAA DIVISION I SLIDING SCALE (Continued)
(2.000 GPA - 2.750 GPA and Above)

Core GPA	SAT Verbal and Math ONLY	ACT *Score
2.750	720	59
2.725	730	59
2.700	730	60
2.675	740-750	61
2.650	760	62
2.625	770	63
2.600	780	64
2.575	790	65
2.550	800	66
2.525	810	67
2.500	820	68
2.475	830	69
2.450	840-850	70
2.425	860	70
2.400	860	71
2.375	870	72
2.350	880	73
2.325	890	74
2.300	900	75
2.275	910	76
2.250	920	77
2.225	930	78
2.200	940	79
2.175	950	80
2.150	960	80
2.125	960	81
2.100	970	82
2.075	980	83
2.050	990	84
2.025	1000	85
2.000	1010	86

* To get an ACT 'composite score', divide the score above by (4)

Appendix E
NCAA Recruiting Chart – Division I and II Football

Academic Year	Division I	Division II
Freshman/Sophomore	No form of contact allowed	No form of contact allowed
Junior	**Recruiting Materials** • Begins September 1 **Telephone Calls** • One Phone call between April 15 and May 31 **Off-Campus Contact** • None allowed until July 1	**Recruiting Materials** • Begins September 1 **Telephone Calls** • Once per week after June 15 **Off-Campus Contact** • June 15 – No more than three off-campus contacts
Senior	**Telephone Calls** • Begins September 1 – Coaches may call once per week* **Off-Campus Contact** • See exceptions below **Official Visit** • Opening day of classes * Unlimited during contact period	**Telephone Calls** • June 15 – Once per week **Off-Campus Contact** • June 15 – limited to three **Official Visit** • Opening day of classes
Evaluations and Contact	Forty-two evaluation days during fall evaluation period (FCS and FBS) • Limit of three off-campus evaluations during an academic year • Not more than six off-campus contacts per prospect at any site, but only one evaluation during fall (Sept./Oct./Nov.) • Two evaluations – April 15 through May 31 (one evaluation to assess athletes ability and one evaluation to assess academic qualifications • FBS head coach; no off campus recruiting, off-campus coaching clinic, visit to a prospective student-athlete's educational institution, or meeting with a prospective student-athlete's coach at an off-campus location during April 15 through May 31 evaluation period • Practice/competition site restrictions	• No restrictions on the number of evaluations • Contact restricted at the site prospect's practice/competition site until such time as the competition has concluded and the prospect has been released by the appropriate authority

The NCAA, "NCAA Recruiting Chart", 2010.

Appendix F

The RDR Recruiting Progression Plan (RPP) - Freshman Year

Completed		Objective/Strategy
Yes	No	
		Read the NCAA's *Guide for the College Bound Athlete*.
		Formulate and set academic and athletic goals.
		Take an ACT/SAT prep class.
		Formulate your recruiting plan.
		Identify core course requirements and ensure you are taking classes that match your high school's list of approved NCAA core courses. **You can receive your school's list of approved core courses at www.eligibilitycenter.org**.
		Maintain at least a 3.0 core grade point average.
		Create and update your highlight film, and player profile throughout the season and again after Spring practice.
		Identify and e-mail twenty-five schools, request school information, provide them with athletic/academic updates and fill out on-line questionnaires.
		Create as many on-line recruiting profile's as possible.
		Identify and visit two to three colleges near you, speak to coaches, arrange a tour if possible.
		Attend at least two combines in the Spring time.
		Attend 7-on-7 competitions in the Summer and at least one or two local Summer football camps that focus on fundamental and skill set development.
		Conduct one transcript credit analysis with your guidance counselor in the month of May and determine the schedule of courses required to graduate eight semesters.
		In the Summer heading into your sophomore year, update your recruiting plan, identify at least fifty schools that match your ability, and send them your highlight film, player profile and fill out on-line questionnaires.
		Seek your head coach's feedback for recruiting tips and strategies for how to improve your skill sets.

Appendix G

The RDR Recruiting Progression Plan (RPP) - Sophomore Year

Completed		Objective/Strategy
Yes	No	
		Take the PSAT and an ACT/SAT prep class.
		Prior to the start of the year: (1) revise your recruiting plan, (2) identify and e-mail at least twenty-five new schools, (3) fill out on-line questionnaires, (4) request school information and (5) provide them with academic/athletic updates.
		Update academic and athletic goals.
		Conduct a transcript analysis immediately after the second term.
		Maintain at least 3.0 a core grade point average.
		Ensure you are taking classes that match your high school's list of approved NCAA core courses.
		Update your highlight film, player profile and on-line recruiting profiles game-to-game, throughout the regular season and after the spring game.
		Identify and visit two to five colleges regionally located near you or within two hundred miles, arrange tours and visit.
		Attend at least two combines in the Spring time.
		Attend 7-on-7 competitions in the Summer and attend a Division I Summer football camp.
		At the conclusion of the playing season: (1) revise your recruiting plan, (2) identify at least fifty new schools that match your ability and (3) send them your highlight film and player profile information.
		Seek your head coach's feedback for recruiting tips and strategies, how to improve your skill sets; as well as, update them on your recruiting goals, efforts and plans.
		Conduct a transcript analysis in May and determine if you are on schedule to graduate in eight semesters.

Appendix H

The RDR Recruiting Progression Plan (RPP) - Junior Year

Completed		Objective/Strategy
Yes	**No**	
		College correspondence begins September 1. Mail back all questionnaires and continue e-mailing interested schools.
		If invited by colleges, attend as many regular season games, Spring Games, or Junior Day events as possible.
		Take the SAT/ACT exam in the Fall and send the scores directly to the NCAA's Eligibility Center (the Eligibility Center's code is **9999**).
		Register for the NCAA Clearing House at www.eligibilitycenter.org.
		Update academic and athletic goals.
		If you have no offers and no interest: (1) revise your recruiting plan, (2) identify at least one hundred new schools that match your ability and (3) send them your updated highlight film and player profile throughout the season.
		Conduct a transcript analysis immediately after the second term.
		Continue to maintain a 3.0 core grade point average.
		Ensure your core classes that match your high school's list of approved NCAA core courses.
		Develop criteria for selecting a college
		Update your highlight film, player profile and on-line recruiting profiles game-to-game, throughout the regular season and after the spring game.
		Attend at least two combines in the Spring time.
		Attend 7-on-7 competitions in the Summer, a Division I Summer football camp, or an "invitation only" showcase camp.
		In the Spring and Summer time: arrange tours and visit schools that are actively recruiting you with your parents.
		Prior to your senior year, meet with your guidance counselor to conduct a transcript analysis. Determine if you are on schedule to graduate in eight semesters and determine all of the courses you need to complete your senior year.
		Have your guidance counselor send your official transcript to the NCAA's Eligibility Center upon completion of your junior year.

Appendix I

The RDR Recruiting Progression Plan (RPP) - Senior Year

Completed		Objective/Strategy
Yes	No	
		Take the SAT/ACT exam in the Fall if necessary.
		If no offers or no interest from schools at the beginning of your senior year: (1) identify between one to two hundred new schools that match your ability, (2) contact them directly and (3) send them your updated highlight film and player profile throughout the season.
		Conduct two (2) transcript analysis: one after the second term and one in May of the fourth term.
		Continue to maintain a 3.0 core grade point average.
		Ensure you are taking classes that match your high school's list of approved NCAA core courses.
		If invited, attend as many regular season games, Spring games, or Junior Day events as possible.
		Develop criteria and narrow down your five college choices.
		Update your highlight film after the third game, then game-to-game as well as your player profile and on-line recruiting profiles.
		Select and attend five official visits if you are not already committed.
		Beginning January 1st, fill out all financial aid forms and all necessary college enrollment applications.
		Request final amateurism certification on or after April first (for fall enrollees) or October first (for Spring enrollees).
		Upon graduation, ensure that your guidance counselor sends your final transcript directly to the NCAA's Eligibility Center with proof of graduation.

Appendix J

Example of a Player Profile

JOE SMITH JR., WR. #9
SOUTHBAY SENIOR HIGH
CLASS OF 2010
HT: 6'2   WT: 195

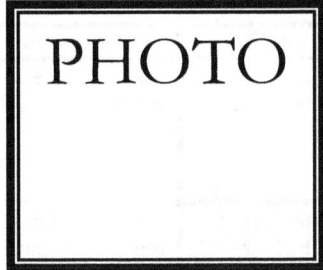

```
┌─────────────────────┐
│                     │
│      PHOTO          │
│                     │
└─────────────────────┘
```

About JOE

Joe is a gifted two-sport athlete who has excelled in both football and in track. Last season Joe led all receivers in receptions and the team in touchdowns. He has all of the tools to be a 'go-to' receiver at the next level, possesses great hands and breakaway speed. In addition, he is a key member of the school's state championship 4 x 4 relay team and is an individual state champion in the 400 meters.

Joe also excels inside of the classroom, as he is academically qualified, maintains a 3.0 core grade point average and is enrolled in all honors courses. Joe is a good-character kid, from a great family, and will be an asset to any program on and off the field.

2010 STATS

- First team All-District and All-State

- Led the team in receptions (50), receiving yards (1000), and TD receptions (16)

- Key senior leader that led the team to a 10-0 regular season record and the state playoffs

- RUSHING YARDS: 250

ACADEMIC INFO

G.P.A: 3.30   **ACT SCORE**: 21
                      SAT SCORE: 950

CLEARINGHOUSE ID: 0906010245

Counselor: Mary John (111) 222-6000 ext. 2248

SCHOOL INFO

Southbay Senior High
12444 SW 200 Avenue
Anywhere, USA 33399
(111) 222-6000
Fax (111) 222-6000

Head Coach:
Kurt Brown (111) 555- 4444

JOE'S CONTACT INFO:

Home Address:
12345 S.W. 900 Terrace
Southbay, USA 33399
Cell # (111) 999-6694
Email: joesmith@mail.com

Appendix K

Student Loan Reference Table

Loan Type	Repayment	Loan Details	Annual Amounts
Federal Perkins Loan	Loan must be repaid	5% loans for both undergraduate and graduate; payment is owed to the school that made the loan	$5,500 maximum for undergraduate students; no minimum award amount
Subsidized FFEL or Direct Stafford Loan	Loan must be repaid; you must be at least a half-time student	U.S. Department of Education pays interest while borrower is in school and during grace and deferment periods	$3,500 to $8,500 depending on grade level
Unsubsidized FFEL or Direct Stafford Loan	Loan must be repaid; you must be at least a half-time student	Borrower is responsible for interest during life of the loan; financial need is not a requirement	$3,500 to $20,500,depending on grade level (includes any subsidized amounts received for the same period)
FFEL or Direct PLUS Loan	Loan must be repaid	Available to parents of dependent undergraduate students enrolled at least half time	Maximum amount is cost of attendance minus any other financial aid the student receives; no minimum award amount

Appendix L

Four-Year Training Log

		HT.	WT.	40 TIME	BENCH PRESS	SQUAT	POWER CLEAN
FRESHMAN	Fall						
	Spring						
SOPHOMORE	Fall						
	Spring						
JUNIOR	Fall						
	Spring						
	SENIOR						

Appendix M

Recruiting Contact Log

Name _____

Address _____

_____

Email _____

Phone: _____ **Fax** _____

Name _____

Address _____

_____

Email _____

Phone: _____ **Fax** _____

Name _____

Address _____

_____

Email _____

Phone: _____ **Fax** _____

Name _____

Address _____

_____

Email _____

Phone: _____ **Fax** _____

Name _____

Address _____

_____

Email _____

Phone: _____ **Fax** _____

Name _____

Address _____

_____

Email _____

Phone: _____ **Fax** _____

Moving the Chains: A Parent's Guide to High School Football Recruiting

Name _____

Address _____

_____

Email _____

Phone:_____ **Fax** _____

Name _____

Address _____

_____

Email _____

Phone:_____ **Fax** _____

Name _____

Address _____

_____

Email _____

Phone:_____ **Fax** _____

Name _____

Address _____

_____

Email _____

Phone: _____ **Fax** _____

Name _____

Address _____

_____

Email _____

Phone: _____ **Fax** _____

Name _____

Address _____

_____

Email _____

Phone: _____ **Fax** _____

NOTES

www.ingramcontent.com/pod-product-compliance
Lightning Source LLC
Chambersburg PA
CBHW060116050426
42448CB00010B/1884